PRAISE FOR *GOD'S ELECT*

God's Elect is a wonderful book that challenges the constructs of both Calvinist and Arminian theologies that have existed for centuries. It has been masterfully written and will force the reader to consider an alternative approach to resolving the inherent challenges within both schools of thought. After serving in ministry with Pastor John Chipman for nearly a decade, I have been fortunate to witness his sincere faith in God and his extreme diligence in researching this matter. His ideas are thought provoking and will cause the reader to examine God's sovereignty, contrasted with our human free will through a different set of lenses.

—**Bob Cote**

GOD'S ELECT

THE
CHOSEN
GENERATION

by
JOHN E. CHIPMAN

Deep River
B O O K S

God's Elect: The Chosen Generation
Copyright © 2022 by John E. Chipman

Published by Deep River Books
Sisters, Oregon
www.deepriverbooks.com

Cover design by Jason Enterline

ISBN—13: 9781632695727
Library of Congress Control Number: 2022901378

Printed in the USA
2022—First Edition
30 29 28 27 26 25 24 23 22   10 9 8 7 6 5 4 3 2 1

TABLE OF CONTENTS

ACKNOWLEDGMENTS

Thanks to my wife, Nancy, who endured, supported,
and loved beyond measure.

Thanks to my son, Johnny, a true "overcomer" whose strength
of spirit is an inspiration.

INTRODUCTION

The mysteries of election, predestination and the divine sovereignty... prying into them may make theologians but it will rarely make saints.

—A.W. Tozer

I believe in God the Father, God the Son, and God the Holy Spirit. I believe that Jesus is the Son of God, the Lord of heaven and earth. I believe that Jesus took on flesh, lived on the earth, and died on a cross to make atonement for our sins so that those who live might live for Him. I believe that He was resurrected on the third day, ascended to heaven, and is at the right hand of the Father, making intercession to save those who draw near to God through Him. In other words, I am a Christian. And so are you, if you believe like I believe.

This means that we are the true children of God, the followers of Jesus Christ. We are justified by faith, loved by God, coheirs of the heavenly kingdom, and no longer slaves to sin. We've experienced the power of the Holy Spirit, tasted the goodness of the word of God, and have assurance of our eternal destinies. We're free, forgiven, and blessed.

But I'm not one of the elect. And neither are you.

I know this might come as a bit of a shock to many of you, and I completely understand the emotional uproar such a statement might elicit. I too have felt my pulse quicken, my hands get clammy, and my world spin as the very foundation of my faith became unstable and my understanding of the nature of God was challenged by the implications of the doctrine of divine election.

A wise pastor once told me that wrestling with the concepts of election and predestination was a kind of rite of passage for all serious Christians. He went on to comment that, at some point, everyone must come to their own understanding of how to deal with the clear passages in Scripture that seem to say that a sovereign God chooses people to use for his purposes and to lavish his love and grace upon, while others are "passed over" (a nicety for "predestined for hell").

This wise pastor was right. The biblical doctrine of election and predestination is the single most emotionally challenging theological concept in Scripture. While there are certainly other enigmatic doctrines (the Trinity and the hypostatic union come to mind), a person's eternal destiny and spiritual well-being do not hinge on whether you understand how God is one-in-three persons (the Trinity), or in knowing how Jesus could be 100 percent God and 100 percent man (hypostatic union). But a doctrine which posits that a person's eternal destiny depends on whether they have been chosen by God for salvation or not is worth understanding correctly. Warren Wiersbe, the well-known Bible commentator, tells of a seminary professor who once said to him, "Try to explain the doctrine of election and you may lose your mind. But try to explain it away and you may lose your soul!"[1] Indeed, a doctrine in which both our standing in eternity and the very nature of the

God we worship hang in the balance is a doctrine worth serious contemplation.

So, contemplate I did—just as scholars, theologians, and philosophers have done for more than two thousand years. For more than a decade I wrestled with some very personal implications of this biblical doctrine. Then one day, while reading the short and oft-overlooked letter written by the apostle John to "the elect lady and her children" (2 John 1), a thought—more like an inspiration, a prompting—occurred to me that within this letter there is a suggestion of something really important, something that would help unlock a correct understanding of the doctrine of election as it relates the gospel of grace.

This book makes no claim to be deeply philosophical or scholarly. The arguments are intentionally simple, yet profoundly biblical. While I greatly respect the scholarship and the depth of research of many others who have tackled this subject, I wanted to present a few ideas that I have not seen explored in any of the mountains of research I've reviewed on the topic. It is my hope that you will recognize and benefit from some original biblical insights into the doctrine of election and predestination. In the end, the real purpose of this book is to share a journey that began with an all-too-common spiritual naiveté, passed through some dark and stormy doctrinal seas, and finally arrived at a beautiful sunlit meadow of clarity and peace and hope, a place where a faithful, loving, and just God reigns—the true God of the Bible.

Common Ground

I sincerely hope that this new perspective on a somewhat perplexing topic is encouraging to all Christians willing to let God's word speak for itself. However, there are a few basics that we all must share to ensure that we're starting from the same benchmark. Here are three things we must affirm:

1. *Every Christian wants to get this right.* Every serious disciple of Jesus wants to understand God, God's plan, God's purpose, and our purpose *in* God's plan. We all want what God wants, but we acknowledge with humility that there will always be mysteries associated with God—and also acknowledge with humility that God himself is often inscrutable. We must accept the things he has declared yet has chosen not to reveal clearly; but we must also acknowledge, explore, and seek to understand without prejudice the things that he has made plain.

2. *If the Bible says it, we believe it.* We can understand much about God on the basis of his own self-disclosure in his creation, in his word as revealed to us in our Bibles, and in the person of Jesus Christ. While we must affirm the veracity of the Bible as the word of God, we must also acknowledge the interpretive nature of language. Having said that, it is important that we let the Bible speak for itself. We must resist manipulating the text. We must resist altering verb tenses, adding words, or redefining terms. We must let the Scriptures inform our theology, resisting the temptation to overlay a predetermined ideology or presupposed mindset onto them.

3. *The Bible is accessible and noncontradictory.* "I thank you... that you have hidden these things from the wise and understanding and revealed them to little children; yes, Father, for such was your gracious will" (Matt. 11:25–26). The Bible was not written to conceal God's truth but to reveal it. It was not intended to be so cryptic, shrouded, mysterious, or/and secretive that only the cleverest among us could interpret it. And the Bible does not contradict itself. If we encounter

what seems to be a contradiction in the Scriptures, we must assume error on our part, not a contradiction on God's part.

Test All Things

What's presented here is not a traditional viewpoint. I encourage you to be skeptical and discerning. In an ages-old religion, "non-traditional" is always suspect, and rightfully so. I fully expect this fresh look at the doctrine of election to be challenged by many in certain theological circles—because what I see so clearly in the Scriptures is a departure from much of the traditional thinking on this subject, and because change will always be a bit uncomfortable for many. But, as George Bernard Shaw once said, "All great truths begin as blasphemies." I believe that the truth regarding election is not Calvinistic, nor is it Arminian. The truth is simply, well, biblical.

I've included a chapter I've called "Yeah, But What About...?" In these pages I have tried to anticipate the arguments, concerns, and objections from Calvinists, Arminians, traditionalists, and everyone in between, by looking at some popular sections of Scripture commonly debated in the discourse on the topic of election. While my brief exegesis of these passages is not intended to be comprehensive, the testing and validation of this understanding of election was an important part of the process of coming to terms with this puzzling doctrine. I wanted to ensure that my interpretation of God's divine plan of election could be biblically defended and would stand up to the scrutiny of ardent critics. It does.

I've also included a chapter called "Reverberations," in which I explore the ramifications of this new perspective on the doctrine of election and predestination with regard to other commonly held biblical doctrines. I realized that the acceptance of the view proposed here will necessarily require a reexamination of some traditional thinking regarding some commonly held soteriological (salvational) passages and will shed some new light on the much-debated doctrines of eternal security and total depravity. You will find these thoughts in Chapter Seven.

Encouragement

If you have struggled with this doctrine as I have, have found much of the scholarly debate on the topic to be frustratingly confusing and overly (and conspicuously) "highbrow" to the point of near incomprehensibility, and been vexed by the theologians who twist and turn the words of Scripture until familiar biblical passages are barely recognizable, then I hope this noncontradictory, true-to-Scripture understanding of the doctrine of election helps bridge the ages-old disconnect that has divided well-meaning, truth-seeking Christians for centuries.

If you feel like you're caught in an ever-darkening doctrinal bog of election and predestination, and feel like you've lost God somewhere along the way—the God you knew as a child, the God who is gracious and merciful, patient and loving—I hope this effort helps you find your way back to the sunlight, back to solid ground, back to the true God of the Bible.

1

WHAT HAPPENED TO GOD?

The secret things belong to the LORD our God, but the things that are revealed belong to us and to our children forever, that we may do all the words of this law. (Deuteronomy 29:29)

Whenever I encounter a passage of Scripture that I find confusing, cryptic, or incongruous, I mark it with a boxed X in the margin of my Bible. For the time being, I tuck it away in my "junk drawer"—a mental storage place where I put things that I don't know what to do with. But they don't go away. Every time I open my Bible, there they are. Like the junk drawer in my house, every time I open the drawer all the "junk" is still there, and I still don't know what to do with it.

For many years, my Bible "junk drawer" has been filled with things that many theologians refer to as "tensions," "mysteries," or "paradoxes"—all polite terms to avoid the word "contradictions," because all would agree that the Bible does not—indeed, cannot—contradict itself. I'm convinced that some of these "junk drawer" items in my Bible are truly the secret things that belong to the Lord (Deut. 29:29) and that we will never understand them completely until the next life when we no longer "see in a mirror dimly." I'm content to let these things remain unresolved.

Aha!

Over the years, however, I have been able to find the proper place for some of the odds and ends from the drawer. Over time, some of the "mysteries" have been solved, some of the "paradoxes" eliminated, some of the "tensions" relieved. This usually happens in a moment of revelation—an "Aha!" moment that leaves me in awe of God's plan and scratching my head wondering why I wasn't able to grasp the now-obvious meaning sooner.

These moments of clarity are usually accompanied by a sense of giddiness bordering on euphoria. I suspect the apostles experienced a similar feeling when, on their final night with Jesus, the light finally went on and they at last understood what Jesus had been trying to teach them for the past three years. We can sense their excitement when they suddenly say to Jesus, "Ah, now you are speaking plainly and not using figurative speech!" (John 16:29). I imagine a fatherly smile coming across Jesus's face as he said to them, "Do you now believe?" (vs. 31). Similarly, as I experience one of my "Aha!" moments, I can almost sense God smiling wryly and saying to me, "Ah, do you now understand?"

One such item that I have come to see clearly and have eliminated from my Bible junk drawer is the doctrine of divine election. After more than a decade of personal struggle, the pieces of this rather perplexing doctrine finally began to fall into place. I have reached an understanding that is noncontradictory and biblically sound. I can't begin to tell you how satisfying it was to be able to page through my Bible and scratch out the boxed Xs next to a whole bunch of verses related to the doctrine of election and predestination.

Victory, right? Well, yes and no. The problem is that my understanding doesn't align with any of the theologians, philosophers, and
scholars who, over the centuries, have endeavored to interpret this
doctrine, many of whom I greatly admire. Believe me, I understand
how tenuous that renders my position. My only source of solace is
the fact that after two thousand years of debate, there has been no
consensus. Scholarly men and women with good intentions and firm
convictions have been labeled heretics, thrown out of the church,
and burned at the stake for expressing an unpopular view of this
doctrine. Arguments have been made. Volumes have been written.
Theories have been proposed. Yet there is still no consensus. So, I
thought, what have I got to lose?

Here, it might be helpful to explain a bit of the backstory.

Stacking the Deck

*And he made from one man every nation of mankind to
live on all the face of the earth, having determined allotted
periods and the boundaries of their dwelling place, that they
should seek God, and perhaps feel their way toward him and
find him. Yet he is actually not far from each one of us. (Acts
17:26–27)*

Acts 17:26–27 is one of my favorite passages of Scripture. I once
heard a well-known and much-admired local pastor paraphrase the
passage this way; "God arranges things in our lives—people, places,
events—to give us our best chance of finding him." In other words,
God stacks the deck for us. He wants us to succeed in our journey to
find the true spiritual treasure—an authentic, satisfying relationship
with our Creator and an unwavering sense of our value and purpose
in his kingdom. As I reflect on the circumstances leading up to my

search for clarity regarding the doctrine of election, there was definitely a bit of "deck-stacking" on God's part.

Like many of us, my church experience was devoid of any notion of a Calvinistic doctrine of election. The first time I heard the term "Calvinism" was in an adult Sunday school class when someone made a passing reference to it. When I asked the leader of the group to explain it he mumbled something about God choosing only some people to save, then quickly moved to another topic, knowing that a discussion of election and predestination could quickly derail the scheduled focus of the class.

Some years later I began attending a Reformed church whose senior pastor was a well-respected Bible teacher, a trusted expositor of the Bible. Over the next several years a Calvinistic view of salvation began to reveal itself. I started to see the many passages in Scripture expressing man's depraved condition and God's sovereign election of certain groups and individuals. I began to see evidence that certain people were chosen by God to receive the saving grace needed to overcome their spiritual deadness, to recognize Jesus as the Messiah and to respond to the gospel message. I started to consider that perhaps, despite years of attending various churches in various denominations, I never correctly understood the Bible, Christianity, the gospel, or the Christian God. This "choosing" seemed to be an integral part of God's plan. So, like many before me, desiring that God's will be done here on earth as it is in heaven, I became a reluctant Calvinist.

It Gets Personal

During those same years, our teenage son began to struggle with drug addiction. He dropped out of high school during his sophomore year. His eyes became dark and vacant. His attitude became defiant and combative. His wholesome, respectable friends were replaced by new friends of questionable character. He became involved in gang-related criminal activities and spent a couple of stints in juvenile hall. He had been arrested multiple times by the time he was nineteen years old. The final arrest was for six "strike-able" felonies at a time when California had the infamous "three strikes" law. Upon a person's third strike, the law mandated an automatic twenty-five-years-to-life sentence. However, since our son's six felonies were concurrent, the court charged him with two strikes and sent him to prison.

A New Ministry

What I just described in a single paragraph is a very abbreviated account of an incredibly challenging ten-year ordeal for my wife and me. However, during that time, the Reformed church we were attending announced that it was forming a new ministry. They were putting together a team to conduct church services for the inmates in the local county jails. We attended a meeting, raised our hands, and became part of the jail ministry team.

For the next several years, at least one Sunday each month, my wife and I would minister to the incarcerated men and women in the local jails. Each Sunday, our team would be escorted through the catacombs of the facility hallways to our assigned module. We would arrive early enough to set up the chairs, organize the classroom, and pray. Then we would wait for the inmates to be escorted to the room.

As the men (or women) came in wearing yellow or orange jumpsuits, we would stand at the door, smile, and warmly welcome them. Many were covered from the tops of their shaved heads to the tips of their fingers with tattoos. Some walked with a swagger, some looked scared, some smiled, some scowled. Most were obviously gang-affiliated. Yet all came voluntarily, of their own accord. I'm sure there were some who were just looking for an opportunity to get out of their cells for an hour, but I sincerely believe that the majority were drawn by a God-given sense that something was broken in their lives. I'm convinced that these meetings were divine appointments arranged by a loving God so that these struggling souls would *seek him, reach out for him and perhaps find him, though he was not far from each one of them* (Acts 17:27).

One day, as I stood in front of a group of young men with my prepared message, ready to offer them a chance to experience a love beyond understanding and to find hope and grace and mercy and joy and purpose, I could see the face of my own son in each of them. No doubt they too, have broken-hearted mothers and fathers who had great hopes for their children and who were struggling to understand where it all went so wrong. Yet what I saw in the faces of these young men was not the vacant stare of drug addicts or the hardened countenance of career criminals but the faces of lost children—the kind of lost children the Bible tells us God cares for, searches for, and rejoices over when they are brought back into the fold.

As we witnessed to these inmates month after month, I had a profound sense of gratitude for all the other church volunteers who love and care and minister to those in prison. Perhaps someone, somewhere was reaching out to my son, inviting him to enjoy the grace and forgiveness of God through the love of Jesus Christ.

Something's Not Right

While there was great satisfaction in serving God in this ministry, a conflict was beginning to stir within me. There were two questions that my newfound Reformed theology suddenly made personally consequential:

1. Did Jesus die for these young men? (Did Jesus die for my son?)

2. Does God love these young men? (Does God love my son?)

Initially, I sought the answers from several Reformed teachers and pastors. The answer I got to the first question above was simply, and matter-of-factly, "Not necessarily. Jesus died only for *his* people, those given to him by the Father—the elect."

The answer I was given to my second question was a bit more complicated. One response from a number of Reformed sources was again simply and matter-of-factly, "Not necessarily. God doesn't love everyone." However, one local pastor assured me that God loves everyone, but just not in the same way. "Some people," he said, "God loves with a special, saving love, but he loves everyone with common grace, providing things like sunshine and rain, but not necessarily granting the salvific love necessary for eternal life." He then presented as an illustration the difference between his love for his wife and his love for the other women of the church. He certainly loves them both, he assured, but commented on how "weird" it would be if he loved the other women of the church in the same way he loved his wife.

The implications of the Calvinistic doctrine of divine election suddenly became personal and quite unsettling. I began to understand what the apostle Paul describes as God's Spirit testifying with our spirit (Rom. 8:16). Every fiber of my being cried out, "Something isn't right!" What about my son? Does God love him? Well, not necessarily. Did Jesus die for him? Well, not necessarily. I was deeply troubled. Indeed, something wasn't right.

This was the beginning of a decades-long search to grasp the truth about God's love, and justice, sovereignty, and plan. In short, it stirred in me a passion to really understand the God of the Bible, and specifically his doctrine of election and predestination. Looking back on the timing and circumstances leading up to this point—my move to the Reformed church, my son's struggles with drugs, my involvement in the jail ministry, the stirring of my spirit—it was obviously the work of God "stacking the deck" to lead me here.

What About Love?

> *Why did God give [man] free will? Because free will, though it makes evil possible, is also the only thing that makes possible any love or goodness or joy worth having... the happiness which God designs for his higher creatures is the happiness of being freely, voluntarily united to Him and to each other in an ecstasy of love and delight compared with which the most rapturous love between a man and a woman on this earth is mere milk and water.[2]*

—C. S. Lewis

In the midst of my personal turmoil regarding the Reformed view of God's plan for salvation, an issue came up one morning in my men's Bible study group regarding God's sovereign choice of all who would be saved, and who would not. One astute but soft-spoken young man in the group quietly asked, "What about love?"

The question hung in the air for an uncomfortable number of seconds, followed by a gradual ramping up of some lively discussion about the meaning of love and the sovereignty of God. Is it really love if it isn't freely given? Is God really sovereign if he doesn't control every event in his world? After fifteen minutes or so, the discussion ended with a common Reformed rebuke from some of the group leaders to the tune of, "Who are you, O man, to answer back to God? Who are you to question Almighty God's plan for salvation? We're all deserving of hell and should be thankful that God, in his grace, chose to save *anyone*."

A Really Good Question

And yet, "What about love?" struck me as a really good question. As I was struggling to come to terms with the Reformed concept that God might not love my son—or at least, that he might not have chosen my son to be one of his—I pondered the illustration the Reformed pastor gave about how he loves his wife one way and loves the other women of the church in another way (an illustration I've heard a number of times since). I thought, "Yeah, but there's a huge difference—the pastor might not love all the women of the church in the same way he loves his wife, but I doubt that pastor wills eternal misery upon the other women of the church." Yet, that's the Calvinistic view of God's will for the nonelect.

John Wesley, upon reflecting on the Calvinist view of God's "love" for the nonelect, once pondered, "Is not this such a love as makes your blood run cold?" [3] In truth, such a "love" as described above does not resemble any concept of love I have ever known. What manner of love intentionally wills misery? I began to wonder: If my understanding of divine love was so far afield, was God's justice also incomprehensible to me? How about his truth? His goodness? The list of foundational insecurities that began to unravel my traditional understanding of Christianity went on and on. I needed to know, is the Reformed understanding of God representative of the real God of the Bible? Is the Reformed concept of divine election true?

The Puzzle

Uncovering the truth behind the somewhat enigmatic doctrine of election and predestination was like putting a jigsaw puzzle together. The first step is just getting all the pieces out of the box and onto the table where they can be clearly examined. Then you've got to take the time to turn them face up, rotate them, and arrange them so that the unique properties of each piece can be thoroughly scrutinized. Finally, you need to determine how each piece relates to the rest of the puzzle and what role it plays to form the big picture.

I began to pour through the Scriptures, highlighting every verse that seemed to reference, even remotely, the doctrine of election. One method of study that was especially helpful was the commitment to memorize every passage of Scripture that I found difficult to fully grasp. Whenever I encountered something particularly perplexing, I would commit it to memory. This required the repetition of many passages over and over again—twenty, thirty, forty times, maybe more. I once read where, on the average, a passage must be repeated fifty-seven times for a person to really "own" it. Fifty-seven times! And that's the *average*! This strategy led me to memorize not only many of the key scriptures related to election, but entire chapters of the Bible. I found that when we place such dedicated focus on God's word, he will often honor our commitment with a deeper understanding of a passage's meaning and purpose.

Although the Bible was my primary resource, I read just about everything I could get my hands on—books, essays, blogs, articles. I listened to debates, lectures, and radio discussions. I sought ideas, counsel, and opinions from wise and trusted mentors. And of course, I prayed, meditated, and studied. In the beginning, the journey produced more questions than answers. For every verse that seemed to support the Calvinistic understanding, there was a verse that seemed to contradict it. For every verse that expressed exclusivity in salvation, there was a verse that seemed all-inclusive. For every verse that expressed God's sovereignty in election, there was a verse that held people accountable for their own faith and a responsibility to repent and believe.

In seeking to resolve these and a myriad of other conundrums, I found it especially frustrating that in theological circles many scholars took great pride in their ability to skillfully "spin" passages of Scripture. They often cited the original Hebrew, Greek, Latin, or Aramaic; or syntax, grammar, or lexicography—manipulating the verses until they appeared to support their theological positions. As I read through volumes of commentaries on the various understandings of divine election, it seemed that many of the scholars were less interested in clarifying the difficult passages and more interested in convincing the reader/listener that the Scriptures aren't really saying what you think they're saying.

While I don't deny that the knowledge the ancient languages and the appropriate application of language arts can be helpful to discern the intended meaning of biblical texts, the apostle Paul warned of the misuse of such oratorical sophistry, and defended his own plain, simple speech:

> For Christ did not send me to baptize but to preach the gospel, and not with words of eloquent wisdom, lest the cross of Christ be emptied of its power. (1 Corinthians 1:17)

> And I, when I came to you, brothers, did not come proclaiming to you the testimony of God with lofty speech or wisdom. (1 Corinthians 2:1)

> For we are not, like so many, peddlers of God's word, but as men of sincerity, as commissioned by God, in the sight of God we speak in Christ. (2 Corinthians 2:17)

Paul knew the persuasive power of highfalutin' rhetoric. He feared that the ability to skillfully manipulate the language, or to speak and write with a kind of rhetorical flourish, would nullify the power of the cross and blur the beauty of the gospel of grace.

The Final Straw

Yesterday upon the stair,
I met a man who wasn't there
He wasn't there again today
I wish, I wish he'd go away.
                    —William Hughes Mearns

Colorless green ideas sleep furiously
                    —Noam Chomsky

John Piper, a leading advocate of Calvinism, asserts, "If you're willing to live with mystery, there's a glorious freedom in taking the Bible for what it says."[4] He goes on to say that as Christians we must have "a capacity for mystery" if we are to allow God to speak to us through his word. While there are certainly plenty of mysteries surrounding the workings, wonders, and nature of the God of the Bible, it seemed as if the Reformed doctrine of election was inventing new ones—and in doing so, was morphing the majesty of the Christian God into something hideous. The hideousness of the Reformed god—that was the final straw.

Tension. Mystery. Paradox. As mentioned earlier, these words are Reformed euphemisms for contradictions that the Reformed understanding of the doctrine of election can't resolve. In addition to my struggle to come to terms with the Calvinistic view of God's "love," there were other issues I couldn't reconcile in my mind. For example, the law of noncontradiction states that something cannot be true and untrue in the same sense, at the same time. An idea cannot be colorless and green. We cannot meet a man who doesn't exist. A person cannot have the freedom to choose if God has predetermined his choice... or can he? And a person for whom God did not grant the ability to believe cannot be justly punished for his unbelief... or can he?

These challenges regarding the sovereignty and justice of God are just some of the difficulties with the Calvinistic doctrine of election and predestination. All Christian scholars agree that the Bible cannot contradict itself. So, the real problem is what to do when a doctrinal overlay on the Scriptures *creates* the apparent contradictions. When a contradiction can't be manipulated into plausibility by linguistic contortions, the final resort seems to be an appeal to "mystery," "tension," or "paradox."

John MacArthur, a well-known and respected pastor and teacher unable to resolve apparent contradictions caused by Calvinism, addresses the issue of "tension" in the doctrine of election this way: "I'm happy to concede that God can resolve things that I can't." He goes on to say, "In every major doctrine of the Bible you have an apparent paradox that you can't resolve. I know that I'm kept eternally secured by God, but I also know I'm commanded to persevere in faith. I know I can't be saved unless I'm chosen and called. And I know I can't be saved unless I'm willing to repent and believe. I don't have to harmonize it. But nor can I deny those things. You rest in the fact that you don't need to grasp the mysteries that are clear in the mind of the eternal God."[5]

In other words: John MacArthur, like many of the Reformers, disagrees with C. S. Lewis who said, "Nonsense remains nonsense even when we talk it about God."[6] In Reformed theology, God can do nonsense, apparently.

Very Strange

In the popular Netflix series *Stranger Things*, there exists a parallel world, an "upside down world." The upside-down world is similar in its general form to the real world of color and life, light and warmth, but it is dark and murky, filled with dread and despair. The upside-down world is ruled by a monstrous creature who enters the real world through a portal—a hole in the temporal fabric that separates the two worlds. The creature inhabits people, changing their genetic structure, making them part of a larger organism under the control of the monster. Of course, the monster is evil.

One of the solid rocks on which we stand in Christianity is that God cannot act contrary to his nature. God is love; he cannot do hate. God is light; he cannot do dark. God is just; he cannot do injustice. God is good; he cannot do evil. I suppose that God did not have to be this way. He could have been anything he desired but he chose to be true and faithful, merciful and gracious, patient and loving. He chose to be a God we can depend on, a God we can trust. If anyone's god is contrary to these qualities, we must reject him. He is not the God of the Bible. If anyone's doctrine promotes a god who is contrary to these qualities, we must reject it. The doctrine is sub-Christian. We can call a doctrine in which God predetermines eternal misery for the vast majority of his creation, "loving"... but it's not. We can claim that a doctrine in which God punishes people for the sins he determined for them to commit "just"... but it's not. We can deny that it's a contradiction to say that "every choice we make is free and every choice we make is determined."[7] We can even give it a fancy name like "compatibilism," but it's still a contradiction. And we can call a doctrine in which God is indistinguishable from the devil a "doctrine of grace"... but it's not.

Nonsense

Nonsense is nonsense even when we use it to talk about God. If God could do nonsense, beneath our spiritual feet is not a rock at all but unstable, shifting sand. Can anyone really count on and trust a

God who can do nonsense? What does this say about the nature of God? How dependable and trustworthy is the word of God if "grace" is really the opposite of grace, if "love" is really unloving, if God's "justice" is unjust? What kind of creature are we worshipping if our God does not abide by the laws he created and by his own teachings? What do we really have in a god who can act capriciously, apart from his nature if not a god of mythology and whimsy?

There is always the possibility, some argue, that we humans don't really know what divine love is. Maybe we don't quite "get" divine justice or divine mercy or divine goodness or divine righteousness. There is always the possibility, they say, that there is some "greater good" that God is working out and that, at least for now, we can't understand these things. The problem is that God tells us that we *do* know these things. We know them because God put the knowledge of these things in each of us. We know love, we know justice, we know goodness, and we know righteousness. In fact, God requires them of us. In reference to God's command to obey his laws (including the command to be loving, just, good, and righteous), Moses tells the people of God that his commandment for these things "is not too hard for you, neither is it far off" (Deut. 30:11). Love, justice, goodness, and righteousness are not only knowable for us; they are *doable* for us.

The Upside-Down God

After several years in the Reformed church it seemed as if I had fallen through the mysterious portal of Calvinism into the "upside-down world" where nothing is as it seems, where contradictions abound and human beings are just part of a larger organism under the complete control of an evil monster named "God."

This was the last straw for me. When the God who is revealed in the Bible had become unrecognizable—or worse, a corruption and a horror—it was time to seek the truth. Somewhere in the Scriptures was a doctrine of election and predestination that revealed the real God: merciful and gracious, slow to anger and abounding in steadfast love, a God who loves his creation such that he gave his only Son so that all of the "whosoevers" in the world—you and me, the inmates in the jails, my own son—would have a chance at eternal life in fellowship with him.

So I concluded, after years of searching for understanding, that the god of Calvinism was not the God of the Bible. In the next chapter we'll see how their god was born from a distortion of the beautiful, big picture of the gospel—the result of a very basic flaw in their doctrine of election.

2

WHAT'S WRONG WITH THIS PICTURE?

... for I did not come to judge the world but to save the world.
(John 12:47)

My brother and I still laugh about the time the welders in his large manufacturing company decided to go on a work-slowdown strike. After some discussion, all the workers agreed to abide by management's directive to ramp up production— all except one, a man named Robert. After a couple of weeks went by, my brother called Robert into his office where he showed him a large, colorful graph illustrating the production of each individual welder in the plant for the past two weeks. The upswing of each line next to the welders' names showed a dramatic increase in production, for everyone except Robert. The disparity on the graph between those whose production had increased and the one whose didn't was so painfully obvious that all my brother had to do was ask Robert one simple question, "What's wrong with this picture?"

In the last chapter, I concluded that the god of Calvinism is not the God of the Christian Bible. It seems the Reformed doctrine of election had unwittingly transformed the Almighty God into a compassionless, sinister god who creates human beings whom he has rendered hopelessly doomed to eternity in hell—a destiny he predetermined for them before they even came into existence. I found it impossible to reconcile the Reformers' god with the God of Scripture, who takes no pleasure in the death of anyone (Ezek. 18:32), who seeks the lost (Luke 15:4), who shows compassion for those who suffer (Luke 10:33), who comforts those who mourn (Matt. 5:4), and yes, who judges the wicked with righteous judgment (Ps. 9:4). We learned that the Reformers themselves could not reconcile those conflicting natures of their god either. They seemed content to just shrug their shoulders and chalk the contradictions up to tension, mystery, or paradox.

I could not ignore the fact that these human beings, condemned for all eternity by the Reformed god, were just people—flawed people, for sure—but people with beating hearts and viable lives, quickened by God, who are loved and cared for and cherished by other human beings—mothers, fathers, sons, daughters, neighbors, friends. It seemed that while I was struggling to put together my doctrine-of-election jigsaw puzzle so that the picture of the gospel looked like the one on the cover of the box, someone had slipped in some pieces from another puzzle altogether. The cruel thing was, the pieces almost fit. It wasn't until the puzzle was nearly complete that I could tell that the picture that was being created was a grotesque distortion of the beautiful image of the gospel of grace.

But It Seems So Right

That's the subtle yet insidious danger of Calvinism. It seems so right, so logical, so rational. Everything seems to connect together like a string of pearls. All the signposts along the way seem to point in the right direction:

- Man is dead in trespasses and sins, and
- a dead man cannot bring himself to life. Therefore,
- God steps in to quicken those he has chosen.
- Jesus dies to efficaciously make atonement, but only for the elect,
- not losing any but raising them up on the last day.

It's the gospel, they say. It's the "unbreakable golden chain of redemption."[8] God elects, he predestines, he calls, he justifies, he glorifies. It's all God. He gets all the glory.

Although the scope of this discussion is not to offer an exhaustive critique of Calvinism—there are plenty of books that offer such—it always seems like kind of a cheap shot to tell someone they're wrong without offering some explanation. It's easy to fall into the role of a cynic, providing a kind of hit-and-run strategy that we see all too often leveled against Christianity. It's another thing altogether to stick around long enough to explain why they're wrong—and yet another thing still to offer an alternative.

A Short History Lesson

Before explaining what I discovered to be an obvious but often overlooked error with Calvinism, it might be helpful to take a moment to review a bit of church history with regard to election.

The early church fathers almost unanimously believed that election as presented in the New Testament was based on foreseen faith. This is the classic Arminian concept which posits that God, before the foundation of the world, looked into the future to see who would believe. These, they say, are the elect of God, the true Christians.

And those who were foreseen to rebuff God's grace were deemed not worthy of salvation. In short, most early Christians believed that election was based on God's foreknowledge of future human choices.

Sometime in the early fifth century CE (the exact date depends on which scholar you read), a highly respected theologian named Augustine of Hippo saw folly in the widely accepted understanding of election based on God's foreknowledge because it makes man the ultimate "decider" rather than a sovereign God. "Salvation belongs to the Lord" (Jon. 2:9); therefore, man was robbing the sovereign God of his glory by taking credit for God's work in salvation. Augustine proposed a "monergistic" election—that is, the belief that God's choice of who would be saved is not based on anything in the person, including foreseen faith. He proposed that God's choice of who would be saved and who would not was based exclusively on his own will and good pleasure, in what John Calvin referred to as God's "secret counsel." The Augustinian concept of divine election was taken up as one of the principal precepts in the Protestant Reformation of the sixteenth century, led by Martin Luther and later firmly established by Calvin in his publication of *Institutes of the Christian Religion* in 1536.

In 1610 the followers of a theologian named Jacobus Arminius produced a document known as The Five Articles of Remonstrance, in which they expressed disagreement with the teachings of Calvin. Article One of the document rejected the Augustinian notion that election was monergistic and unconditional. They proposed a return to the early church fathers' belief that biblical election unto salvation was conditioned upon foreseen faith. God elects those whom he knows beforehand will believe.

Finally, in 1618, the supporters of Augustinian/Calvinism convened at the Synod of Dort and developed their own five-point rebuttal to counter The Five Articles of Remonstrance. This, in part, included what is now known as the Reformed doctrine of unconditional election. Here is a short, (yet, I believe, accurate) understanding of the Augustinian/Calvinism (Reformed) doctrine of election:

> "All (people) are not created on equal terms."[9] God, from before the foundation of the world, divided all people into two groups; those he chose to save (the elect), and those who were not chosen to save (the nonelect/reprobate). God's choice was not based on anything in the person, including foreseen faith. The elect will go to heaven. The nonelect will go to hell. God's election is unconditional and final.

In summary, according to Reformed doctrine, the fate of every person—you, your children, your neighbors, etc.—has been predetermined by God and while an elect person is guaranteed heaven, there's nothing a nonelect person can do to change God's decree of divine rejection and eternal damnation.

A Fatal Flaw

As I continued to seek the true biblical understanding of the doctrine of divine election, I came to the conclusion that the distortion of the true God of the Bible offered by Calvinism is the result of a fatal flaw in the Reformed version of the gospel. And I believe that the flaw in their understanding of the gospel is partly the result of losing sight of the big picture: the purpose for Jesus's incarnation and the reason for the cross.

A wise Christian scholar will want to constantly check his bearings against the true north of Jesus on the cross to be sure his doctrine hasn't led him down the wrong road. If you can't see the face of

God's love for the world on the cross—the face of an unfathomable love for all mankind—you've lost sight of the big picture.

So where did Calvinism take such a wrong turn? I believe the misstep occurs in the very beginning of their doctrine. The belief that God, from before the foundation of the world, divided all people into two groups, the elect and the nonelect, is not supported anywhere in Scripture. Even worse, it radically contradicts the revealed nature of God. The result of this initial misstep in the Calvinistic understanding of the doctrine of election is that when you reach the road's end, not only do you suddenly realize that the god you have been worshipping has little resemblance to the God of the Bible, but that the Reformed doctrine of election fails to recognize and celebrate the very nature and purpose of the cross. Jesus says, "I did not come to judge the world but to save the world" (John 12:47).

The salvation of the world—that's the big picture. If any model of the gospel doesn't include an opportunity for all of humankind to be saved, we must ask ourselves, "What's wrong with this picture?"

Salvation: A Business Plan

The salvation of a single soul is more important than the production or preservation of all the epics and tragedies in the world.... The glory of God, and, as our only means to glorifying Him, the salvation of human souls, is the real business of life.

—C. S. Lewis[10]

In a very real sense, the Bible is one book written by one author telling one story—God's plan to save the world through his Son Jesus Christ. We could say that the God of Scripture is in the business of saving human souls and what God shares with us in the Christian

Bible is his "business plan." In every business enterprise, the goal is success, and success is generally defined by profitability. The soul-saving business is no exception. God is looking for profit. Nowhere is this clearer than in the "Great Commission," where Jesus tells his apostles to go into the world and make disciples of all nations (Matt. 28:18–20). In its essence, the Great Commission is a command by the boss to his apprentices to grow the business and to be profitable.

The New Testament doctrine of election and predestination is an integral component of God's business plan. In the New Testament, divine election can be described as an apprenticeship program in which God recruits individuals to be trained, mentored, enabled, and commissioned for service in the kingdom, all with the ultimate goal of saving the world. Any doctrine that fails to support God's ultimate desire of saving the world through Jesus Christ cannot be defended as a true biblical teaching.

A Business Lesson

In Chapter 25 of the Gospel of Matthew Jesus told a parable intended to teach his disciples the responsibility of God's apprentices, his chosen servants, to be profitable for the kingdom. When the boss invests time and resources to train up his workers, he expects results. The parable is an illustration of a statement made earlier by Jesus, "Everyone to whom much was given, of him much will be required" (Luke 12:48).

Jesus told of a man going away on a journey, who gives one servant five talents, another two talents, and another one talent. A talent was an exceptionally large sum of money. The servant with five talents invested wisely and returned ten talents to the master. The servant with two talents also doubled what he was given. These two servants are praised as "good and faithful." But the servant who was given one talent buried it in the ground and returned to the master only what he was originally given. For this he is rebuked, and called "wicked" and "lazy" by the master (Matt. 25:14–30).

Note that God (the master) expects his apprentices, those in whom he has invested and gifted with special abilities (talents), to be effective and profitable—that is, to return to him more than they are given, to grow the kingdom, to provide increase. In other words, God, whose business is the redemption of lost souls, expects profit, and profit in the soul-redemption business simply means more saved people. Note also that breaking even is not an option. The chosen servant who gives back to the master only what he was originally given is severely rebuked.

A Really Bad Business Model

With the parable of the talents in mind, let's look at the Augustinian/ Calvinistic view of election and its role in the gospel of Jesus Christ. I've created a simple model to help us better understand the basics of their doctrine of election.

The Father ➡ "The Elect" ➡ Jesus ➡ "The Elect" ➡ The Father

Here's how the model works:

- The Father divides everyone into two groups. He chooses all who will be saved, the elect (Eph. 1:4). All others—the nonelect—are "passed over," not chosen by the Father for salvation.

- The Father gives the elect to Jesus (John 6:37,44, 65). The nonelect are never enabled to believe in Jesus which leaves them in their sins and subject to the righteous judgment of God.

- Jesus gives the elect back to the Father (John 14:6, 1 Cor. 15:24). The nonelect, unable to believe in Jesus, remain in their sins and are condemned.

In its most basic form, the Reformed doctrine of election can be explained like this: In the beginning, the Father chooses people (the elect) to give to the Son. At the end, the Son gives those same people (the elect) back to the Father.

Mr. Augustine, We Have a Problem

I am astonished that you are so quickly deserting the one who called you to live in the grace of Christ and are turning to a different gospel-- which is really no gospel at all. Evidently some people are throwing you into confusion and are trying to pervert the gospel of Christ. (Galatians 1:6–7)

Although there are a number of biblical difficulties with Augustinian-Calvinism, there is one glaring shortcoming revealed by the model that really overshadows the others: it is so obviously contrary to God's plan of salvation so as to nullify the very purpose of the cross. It begs the question: What's wrong with this picture? *In Calvinism, since the Father gets back only those whom he originally chose and gave to Jesus, there's no profit. No increase.*

What we see in this model is a kind of "divine regifting," where Jesus merely repackages the same people who were given to him before returning them to the Father. In view of the parable of the talents, this is the exact result for which a servant is called wicked and slothful by the master. Sure, the elect are sanctified and refined by the Holy Spirit, but the master's complaint in the parable is not the *condition* of the talents returned to him, but the *quantity.* A good harvest should provide fruit that is both ripe and plentiful.

In sum, the Calvinistic model of the gospel does not satisfy or support God's requirement that his servants provide profit, and in view of the ultimate goal of the gospel—the salvation of the world through Jesus—the failed Calvinistic model should give us pause. Throughout the Scriptures, God's purpose of election is designed to promote growth and inclusion. Yet the model exposes the fact that the Reformed doctrine of election is a very exclusive gospel with no provision for kingdom growth.

Any interpretation of the gospel that is not "good news" for the whole world is not the gospel of Jesus Christ which, according to the apostle Paul, is no gospel at all.

3

SO, NOW WHAT?

*[The] wrong path is the right path to gain experience in your
search for the right path!*

—*Mehmet Murat ildan*

So, there I sat. Before me was an unfinished jigsaw puzzle with loose pieces of doctrine of various shapes and colors strewn all over the table in front of me. I knew only that Calvinism failed to produce a biblical picture of the gospel, the "good news" that Jesus came to save the world. The exclusivity of the Reformed view seemed to conflict with the clear, all-inclusive New Testament invitations offered by Jesus for *everyone* to come to him—all who thirst, all who labor, all who hunger for righteousness. Yet I also knew that there were special people in the New Testament—divinely chosen people—who were called according to God's purpose (Rom. 8:28), gifted with divine powers (1 Thess. 1:5), and appointed to eternal life (Acts 13:48).

Filling in the missing pieces of the puzzle all seemed to boil down to finding the biblical answer to a single question, *Who are the elect of the New Testament?* When the apostle Paul said that he "endure[d] everything for the sake of the elect" (2 Tim. 2:10), we can all agree that knowing to whom he is referring and how these people fit into God's plan of redemption is of paramount importance to the gospel. Any reasonable explanation of the New Testament doctrine of election must address this question.

What Do You Mean by That?

Before we look into how the various understandings of the doctrine of election answer the key question, *Who are the elect of the New Testament?* I want to be sure we have a working definition of biblical election.

Greg Koukl, a well-known Christian apologist, often recommends using what he calls "the Columbo method" when defending the Christian faith. It's a simple, nonthreatening tactic that gently challenges a person's beliefs, beginning with a simple question, "What do you mean by that?" The purpose of the question, of course, is to ensure that everyone has the same starting point by clearly defining the terms. Much of the confusion regarding the doctrine of election and predestination comes from confusion regarding the terminology. So let's take a moment to define a couple of key terms and clear up some common misunderstandings.

The verb "to elect," quite simply, means "to choose." These two verbs, "elect" and "choose," are interchangeable in the New Testament. It often seems that the translators just tossed a coin to decide which word to use in which verses.

> Who shall bring any charge against God's elect? (Rom. 8:33)
>
> Who will bring any charge against those whom God has chosen? (Rom. 8:33, NIV)

It is important to note that while the precedent for God choosing individuals and groups of people is as old as Genesis, the New

Testament seems to give God's "purpose of election" a new expression. Things change with the arrival of Jesus (an understatement, for sure). Perhaps the most obvious evidence of this change in the New Testament is the use of the term "elect" as a noun ("the elect"; "God's elect"), or as an adjective ("the elect exiles"; "the elect lady"). This grammatical usage of the word is not found anywhere in the Old Testament. So, although we could correctly say that all God's chosen servants throughout history were elected/chosen by God, the New Testament clearly puts a focus on a special group of individuals who are called "the elect."

Another New Testament distinction is the implication in the Gospels and the Epistles that there is an election which is connected to salvation. This connection is not found anywhere in the Old Testament. A review of the Hebrew Scriptures reveals that the scope of the biblical doctrine of divine election included the choosing of individuals or groups by God to accomplish several purposes. First, we see instances of people throughout the Scriptures being chosen specifically for service in the kingdom—people recruited to carry out God's work here on earth, i.e., priests and prophets. Then, we clearly see God's choosing of individuals to bring forth the Word of God—people chosen to be part of the genetic line of Jesus. But only in the New Testament writings do we see evidence of an election connected to salvation—people designated to be "raise[d]... up on the last day" (John 6:40), and people "appointed to eternal life" (Acts 13:48).

This is not to say that Old Testament heroes, chosen by God, did not achieve salvation. Although we're not directly told so in Scripture we can safely assume, based on God's faithfulness, that the Old Testament saints who were chosen by God and faithful to their calling (Abraham, Moses, et al.) received the gift of eternal life. And likewise, although we're not directly told so in Scripture, we can assume that those who were chosen yet were not faithful to their calling (Judas, et al.) were condemned. However, there's no evidence that God chose anyone in the Old Testament specifically to be saved.

Here's what I believe the writers of the New Testament intended for us to understand when they referred to election: *God's choosing of individuals to receive the gospel and to believe in Jesus as the Messiah.*

One additional definition that might be helpful to this discussion is the use of the word "called" in the New Testament. In my opinion, when the writers of the New Testament refer to "the called" they are referring to "the elect," but with an additional implication: the election of a person by God is also a summons to service in the kingdom. The Bible describes a great responsibility placed on these special servants. We see throughout Scripture that those who were called by God and divinely gifted were held to an extremely high standard of accountability, with significant consequences for failing to use their gifting to advance God's purposes.

Who Are the Elect?

Here are the three common ideological answers to the question, *Who are God's elect?* as depicted in the New Testament writings:

> *Calvinism:* The elect are those people whom God sovereignly chose from before the foundation of the world to be granted belief in Jesus. In other words, they are the true Christians.
>
> *Non-Calvinism* (for the sake of simplicity, I'm grouping the various perspectives of non-Calvinism into two ideologies, Classic Arminianism and Traditional non-Calvinism):
>
> > *Classic Arminianism:* The elect are those people God foresaw from before the foundation of the world who would freely come to believe in Jesus. In other words, they are the true Christians.

Traditional non-Calvinism: Since Jesus is "the elect one," the elect are simply those who, through a free-will choice of faith, are "in Christ." A corollary to this view is the understanding that the church is the elect entity and that people are elect only through their belief in Jesus, thereby becoming part of the church, the body of Christ. Either way, those "in Christ" or those who are part of the church—the elect—are the true Christians.

I propose that the fact that all traditional schools of thought incorrectly believe that the New Testament term "the elect" refers to all true Christians has been one of the primary sources of confusion and contradiction. While the New Testament elect are certainly true Christians, not all true Christians are of the elect. Please keep reading.

Mr. Arminius, We Have a Problem

... test everything; hold fast what is good.
(1 Thessalonians 5:21)

In all my research, I never doubted the sincerity or the noble intent of any of the expositors from either the Calvinist- or the non-Calvinist perspectives. Yet it seemed that while both sides were eager to expose and exploit the obvious errors in the other's interpretations, they were reluctant to deal with some weaknesses in their own arguments. I'm convinced that although each side sincerely believes that their viewpoint is the most true-to-the-Bible exposition of a somewhat complex concept, they have all accepted the notion that divine election is a doctrine which God, in his wisdom, has deemed unnecessary to make perfectly clear in his word—hence, lots of room for debate.

When I began to explore the non-Calvinistic alternatives, I began to understand why the debate regarding election and predestination has gone on for so many years and why the proponents of the various interpretations get so frustrated, with tempers often boiling over and their Christian witness being forfeited as frustration and exasperation get the better of them. In my opinion, even though the non-Calvinists end up with the correct view of the nature of God, they also rely on tortured exegesis of key biblical verses to justify their understanding of the doctrine.

You might have already surmised that my definition of New Testament election as *God's choosing of individuals to receive the gospel and to believe in Jesus as the Messiah*, conflicts with the classic Arminian understanding—the belief that God looks into the future to see who will choose him. Even though the Arminian view was the prevailing theory by the early church fathers until Augustine in the early fifth century CE, I'm convinced that the apostles themselves did not understand election in that way, and there is no evidence in Scripture for that interpretation.

Based on my definition of New Testament election, there are a few key points worth emphasizing, which reveal the errors in the various views:

1. *In New Testament election, the choosing is always by God.* Whenever an Arminian speaks of God's foreknowledge of who would choose to believe in Jesus, the Calvinists get red in the face with frustration, and rightfully so. There is only one verse in the Bible that an Arminian might use to try to defend the assertion that God "looks down the corridors of time" to see who would believe—Romans 8:29:

   For those whom he foreknew he also predestined to
   be conformed to the image of his Son, in order that
   he might be the firstborn among many brothers.

I share the Calvinists' frustration. First, there is no warrant in this verse (or any verse) to support the notion that God looked into the future to foresee anyone's faith, then determined his own choice of the elect based on that knowledge. In the Bible, the foreknowledge of God is always a reference to the fore-choosing, predetermining, or preplanning of God (Acts 2:23, Rom. 11:2, 1 Peter 1:1–2, 20). I believe that Scripture generally supports the Calvinistic assertion that God knows certain events in the future because God has *determined* those future events, including the positive response of the elect to the gospel message. Additionally, I agree with the Calvinists who maintain that the specific reference in this verse is to the foreknowledge of *people*, not faith—*those whom he foreknew.* Paul is saying that there were *people* foreknown (fore-chosen) by God, an understanding clearly supported in Ephesians 1:4: "even as he chose us in him before the foundation of the world, that we should be holy and blameless before him."

The other cause of frustration with the classic Arminian understanding of election is the implication that the future Christian first chooses God, and then God chooses the Christian. Such a relational pattern is never seen in the Scriptures. God's choice never seems to depend on the actions of his creatures. There isn't a single verse, neither Old Testament nor New Testament, that supports such a process of election. While I believe that the Bible affirms that today's Christians choose God, the back-and-forth volley of choosing as proposed by the non-Calvinists —"You chose me, so okay, now I choose you"—seems more like a grade-school playground exchange, and less than apropos for the sovereign God of the universe.

2. *New Testament election is particular.* In the New Testament, a
corporate group called "the elect" is made up of "elect" individuals. In other words, the elect group is only "elect" because
of the elect individuals who comprise it. This is diametrically
opposed to a popular non-Calvinistic view that election is
corporate, and that individuals are only "elect" in their free-
will choice to be part of the corporate body. As I noted, some
non-Calvinists believe that God chose the church as the elect
group, and that individuals are only "elect" when their faith in
Jesus includes them in the body of the church. Again, the New
Testament reveals the choosing of individuals by God inde-
pendent of any choice they make or any action they perform.

In a similar way, my definition of election also refutes the
traditionalist idea that people are elect only as they put their
faith in Jesus, the "elect one." In other words, they maintain
that becoming a Christian is a requirement to be one of the
elect. In the New Testament, the elect are not Christians
until they hear the gospel. Let me say that again—in the
New Testament, *the elect are not Christians until they hear the
gospel.* In the New Testament, people are referred to as "elect"
before they become Christians. Once again, I agree with the
Calvinists that there were specific people chosen by God,
predestined and enabled to receive the gospel message and
to believe. It is their election by God which puts them "in
Christ," not their decision to believe that makes them elect.

3. *New Testament election is not unto salvation.* The definition I
gave for New Testament election stops short of an election
unto salvation. Even though the New Testament (unlike
the Old Testament) seems to draw a connection between
election and salvation, I believe that while the election
of individuals in the New Testament is unconditional,

salvation is always conditioned upon one's persevering faith in Jesus Christ—even for the elect. With all of the New Testament warnings against being deceived and falling away, it is unrealistic to believe that apostasy is impossible, even for the elect. Some scholars would argue that the warnings are one of the ways God ensures that the elect will not fall away. The reasoning is that God has not only determined the perseverance of the elect but also the means by which he will keep them in faith—in this case, through a false sense of fear. I'm not seeing the God of Scripture behaving like a deceptive parent who tells his child that there are monsters under the bed just to keep him from getting up at night. We'll examine the issue of apostasy in more depth in Chapter 7.

Strange Bedfellows

Generally, the non-Calvinists (Arminians and Traditional) believe in the biblical truth of a loving God who desires all to be saved and who has provided the saving grace that is necessary for everyone who is willing to come to repentance and faith in Jesus. Yet, in an attempt to rescue the character of God from the corruption of Calvinism, the non-Calvinists resort to some questionable exegesis of key biblical passages in order to deny some texts which obviously support a Calvinistic interpretation.

It is somewhat surprising to note that despite the significant disagreements from the various sides of the debate on the doctrine of election, all three of the perspectives (Calvinism, Arminianism, Traditional non-Calvinism) arrive at the same basic answer to the key question, "Who are the elect?" They all conclude that the elect of the New Testament is just another name for all true Christians, which is just another name for the church.

I disagree. That's where we're going next.

4

FREEDOM

So Jesus said to the Jews who had believed him, "If you abide in my word, you are truly my disciples, and you will know the truth, and the truth will set you free." (John 8:31–32)

Jesus says, "the truth will set you free." After more than a decade of struggle and frustration in trying to come to a true-to-the-Bible, noncontradictory understanding of the doctrine of divine election—one that paints a beautiful picture of hope and reveals a gracious, compassionate, and loving God—I felt anything but free. Both the Calvinistic- and non-Calvinistic interpretations of this doctrine impose a heavy burden on Christians. The preoccupation with being chosen by God—that is, being one of the elect—is a great weight on many in the Christian community. Yet even that burden pales in comparison to imagining an unredeemable future for our loved ones.

As I reflected on the depth of the love I have for my own son, I remember being deeply saddened by this statement from John Piper as he contemplated the possibility that his Reformed god may have predestined his children for hell.

> But I am not ignorant that God may not have chosen my
> sons for his sons. And, though I think that I would give
> my life for their salvation, if they should be lost to me,
> I would not rail against the Almighty. He is God. I am
> but a man. The potter has absolute rights over the clay.
> Mine is to bow before his unimpeachable character and
> believe that the Judge of all earth has ever and always will
> do right.[11]

This statement gives me great sorrow. There is no freedom in those words. They reflect a desperate theology that has lost sight of the fact that in love, God gave us his son precisely so that our sons, both John Piper's and mine, would not be without hope. I'm not talking about the tenuous, cross-your-fingers hope that maybe they're one of the lucky ones chosen by God—like the hope of winning the lottery. I'm referring to true, biblical hope—the assurance of knowing that with sincere hearts, all of our children could seek God, reach out for him, and find him. It's the assurance in the promise that God is not far from each one of them (Acts 17:27).

As I listened, watched, read, and studied the many highly respected scholars and theologians who presented their various understandings with great conviction, they didn't seem to be free either. Some relied on strained contortions of biblical texts; some showed agitated impatience with those whose views differed; and some displayed a subtle, off-putting arrogance. All of these un-Christ-like behaviors served to belie their outward confidence, and to reveal a deep unrest of their inner spirit. And since, according to Jesus, the product of spiritual truth is spiritual freedom, the fact that we were all in chains was evidence that no one had the truth—not me, and not the biblical scholars.

Christian, but Not Elect?

*And it shall come to pass that everyone who calls on the name
of the Lord shall be saved. (Joel 2:32)*

One day, as I was somewhat idly reading the short letter of 2 John,
a thought crossed my mind. Although all of the letters in the New
Testament are like reading someone else's mail, this letter is unique
in that it seems to be a very personal letter, not written to a group or
a church, but to an individual—a woman. John refers to her as "the
elect lady." Of course, I've read the commentaries of some expositors who believe that "the elect lady" could be a reference to a local
congregation and that "her children" are the believers who are part
of that church. As mentioned earlier, there are some scholars who
believe that election is corporate and not particular—that is, God has
chosen the church, and individuals are only elect by becoming part
of the church body. Yet, the interpretation that John is addressing a
church as "the elect lady" seemed to me to be somewhat incongruous, not fitting with the typical pattern of the other New Testament
greetings, and unfamiliar to the apostle's own writing signature. The
entire letter is worth reading, but here are the applicable passages
(the paragraph divisions are mine):

> The elder to the elect lady and her children, whom I love
> in truth, and not only I, but also all who know the truth,
> because of the truth that abides in us and will be with us
> forever: Grace, mercy, and peace will be with us, from
> God the Father and from Jesus Christ the Father's Son, in
> truth and love.
>
> I rejoiced greatly to find some of your children
> walking in the truth, just as we were commanded by the

Father. And now I ask you, dear lady—not as though I were writing you a new commandment, but the one we have had from the beginning—that we love one another. And this is love, that we walk according to his commandments; this is the commandment, just as you have heard from the beginning, so that you should walk in it. For many deceivers have gone out into the world, those who do not confess the coming of Jesus Christ in the flesh. Such a one is the deceiver and the antichrist....

Though I have much to write to you, I would rather not use paper and ink. Instead I hope to come to you and talk face to face, so that our joy may be complete.

The children of your elect sister greet you. (2 John 1–7, 12–13)

The Revelation

I confess that although I had read this short letter many times before, I never saw anything of real consequence in it. The body of the letter contains a warning against deceivers, and the apostle John cautions the lady not to receive such false teachers. Such admonitions are common throughout the letters of the New Testament. But this time, I noticed something that had not caught my attention before.

It seemed important to John to refer to this lady as "elect." John did not address her as "my little child," "my beloved," or even "my sister in Christ," as might be expected and as he had done in his other letters. The apostle seemed intent on addressing this person with some particular notoriety. He used the word "elect" in the way a person might use a royal title. It is the only place in all of Scripture where an apostle of Jesus Christ singles out an individual, acknowledging her as one uniquely graced in some way by God. This lady was special. She was one of the elect. She was a Christian, but she was also something other.

I noticed too, that even though some of this lady's children were "walking in the truth," John did not refer to them as elect. Some of her children were Christians, for sure, brothers and sisters in Christ, yet the apostle does not refer to them as elect. They are simply "her children." Of course, in and of itself, this is not a definitive sign that her believing children were not among the elect, but the omission of the title for the children seemed intentional—so intentional that John repeated this pattern in the sign-off of the letter where he informed the elect lady that "the children of your elect sister greet you." Once again, the apostle seemed intent on making the distinction that the sister was "elect," whereas the children were not.

What If...?

At first, this subtle rumination was nothing more than a slight blip of interest, but it began to take root and a "theory" began to form in my mind. Why would John make note in his letter that the lady and her sister were "elect" yet even the believing children were not so referenced? Why the two sisters, but not their kids? What if election was a generational thing? Could it be that New Testament election was limited to a single generation? What if the Reformed view of unconditional election was true but only for a select group of first-century individuals? And what about those children who were walking in the truth but not referred to as elect? Could it be that not all Christians are chosen by God? What if, I thought, not all believers are elect?

With these questions in my mind, I formulated a theory, a hypothesis: *The elect of the New Testament were people chosen by God from a single generation, divinely enabled to recognize the gospel as truth and uniquely gifted to launch the church.*

Radical Implications

> *There's two possible outcomes: if the result confirms the hypothesis, then you've made a discovery. If the result is contrary to the hypothesis, then you've made a discovery.*
>
> —*Enrico Fermi*

The Scientific Method of inquiry is an empirical means of testing hypotheses. A person makes a hypothesis based on induction from certain information. Then he derives logical implications from his hypothesis. Finally, he tests the implications by experimentation or observation of empirical evidence. Of course, the Bible is the ultimate Christian testing ground for all things spiritual and all things doctrinal. Based on my hypothesis that the elect were from a single generation of first-century people—contemporaries of the apostles, chosen by God, divinely enabled to recognize the gospel as truth and uniquely gifted by God to launch the church—I came up with three significant implications.

The Wrong Question

The first important implication of the theory is that, when it comes to the New Testament doctrine of election, we have been asking the wrong question. Instead of asking, "Who *are* the elect?" we should have been asking "Who *were* the elect?"

Although we understand and celebrate the timeless wisdom provided by the inspired writings, we also know that not every verse has direct application to the Christian community two thousand years after its writing. It's often said that while the Bible was certainly written *for* us, for our benefit, it was not written *to* us. N. T. Wright notes that "for too long we have read Scripture with nineteenth-century eyes and sixteenth-century questions. It's time to get back to reading with first-century eyes and twenty-first-century questions."

The New Testament is a first-century document. The Gospels describe the life and ministry of the incarnate Jesus. The establishment of the early church is the focus of the book of Acts. The training, edification, and encouragement of new believers is recorded for us in the Epistles. We mustn't lose sight of the fact that the core focus of most of the New Testament is God's revelation to us of the outworking of a "mystery hidden for ages" (Eph. 3:9): the formation and development of the church, the framework for a plan of redemption that would demonstrate the profound love of God for the world he created so long ago.

Admittedly, it's not always easy to distinguish the verses with timeless, universal application for subsequent covenant communities from those which were specific to the first-century audience being addressed. However, I believe that if we lose sight of the first-century context and try to inject our twenty-first-century selves into every verse, we will distort God's intended message and miss the resourceful beauty and clever implementation of God's church-building strategy.

Good Company

The second implication of this departure from the traditional understandings of the doctrine of election and predestination was actually quite comforting. In the introduction to this book I wrote this:

> I believe in God the Father, God the Son, and God the Holy Spirit. I believe that Jesus is the Son of God, the Lord of heaven and earth. I believe that Jesus took on flesh, lived on the earth and died on a cross to make atonement for our sins so that those who live might live

for Him. I believe that He was resurrected on the third day, ascended to heaven and is at the right hand of the Father making intercession to save those who draw near to God through Him.

In other words, I am a Christian. And so are you, if you believe like I believe.

This means that we are the true children of God, the followers of Jesus Christ. We are justified by faith, loved by God, coheirs of the kingdom of heaven, and no longer slaves to sin. We've experienced the power of the Holy Spirit, tasted the goodness of the word of God, and have assurance of our eternal destinies. We're free, forgiven, and blessed.

But I'm not one of the elect. And neither are you.

I admit that the purpose of that introduction was to get your attention, but I also wanted to remind you that being a Christian is no small thing. As Christians, we are rich, indeed. But if the elect of the New Testament were from a single generation of people, contemporaries of the apostles, then you and I are not part of the elect. However, we're in really good company. Since "the elect" is a New Testament reference, none of the Old Testament heroes were part of the elect either—not Abraham, not Isaac, not Jacob, not Joseph, Moses, or David, nor any of the prophets. That's not to say they weren't chosen by God and anointed to carry out his purposes—but they cannot properly be called part of the distinct group of people referred to as "the elect" in the New Testament writings.

Many of the New Testament saints in our Bibles were not part of the elect either. I believe that Mary was, but Joseph wasn't. Timothy was, but Simeon wasn't. Barnabas was, but John the Baptist wasn't. Even the apostles, I believe, were distinct from the group called "the elect." Yet we have every reason to believe that all the abovementioned faithful servants are enjoying eternal life with Jesus. So, the fact that we—you and I—are not of the elect shouldn't really matter. We are Christians, and that is enough.

Free Indeed

The final realization regarding this new understanding of the doctrine of election took a while to sink in. Breaking free from the chains that have bound us for so many years is a difficult process. Just as a person who has been released from prison after decades of incarceration will have trouble coping with and embracing his newfound but unfamiliar sense of freedom, the ramifications of a new understanding of the doctrine of election were difficult to fully grasp and internalize. If New Testament election was restricted to a single generation of first-century individuals, a clever tool used by God to kickstart the church, the implication is an astonishing revelation: *the doctrine of divine election and predestination has no relevant application for us! None!*

This means that all the volumes written, all the debates argued, all the videos, books, blogs, discussions, and infighting regarding who is chosen and how they're chosen is what the apostle Paul referred to as "empty chatter" (1 Tim. 6:20). It means that the traditional views of the doctrine of election and predestination that have been debated for centuries are quite possibly some of the deceptions and false teachings that we are warned about by the apostle Paul and others as causing division in the body. It means that we have created, nurtured, and allowed to fester an unbiblical malignancy in our midst that has not only caused much needless personal anxiety but, in my opinion, has done great damage to the Christian witness—and all for naught. In other words, the truth that the doctrine of election in the New Testament was unique to a very special group of first-century believers means that we are free: free to choose Jesus, free to believe the gospel, free to love, free to call on the name of the Lord. We are free, indeed.

A Fine Mess

You did not choose me, but I chose you. (John 15:16)

Before we leave this chapter to explore a new model of the gospel and the scriptural justification for my assertion that the elect of the New Testament were chosen by God from a single generation of people, divinely enabled to recognize the gospel as truth and uniquely gifted to launch the church, I want to take a moment to explain why I think we got this issue so wrong for so long.

Everyone likes to be chosen. I remember when I was in the third grade, my class would play kickball a couple of times a week for PE. The teacher would select two captains, who would then stand in front of the classroom and begin choosing teammates. As each student was called, they would get up from their desks and stand behind the captain who chose them. Invariably one girl, Karen, was always the last one still seated at her desk. She was a sweet girl but possessed no athletic abilities. She was a "sure out" every time she came to the plate and everyone knew that they would always get on base if they kicked the ball in her direction. That poor girl must have died a thousand deaths twice a week for an entire school year.

Most of us have experienced the brutal childhood ritual of choosing teams. Most of us have felt the pain of waiting to be chosen, wanting to be chosen, hoping to be chosen. Being chosen was really an affirmation of our worth, our value in the eyes of the chooser. And many of us have experienced the disappointment, embarrassment, and public humiliation of being chosen last. We often look back on it as a kind of rite of passage of childhood. It's one of the ways we learn to accept disappointment, we reason. As hard as it was to be the last one chosen for something, at least we were still chosen. We were still on the team. But not being chosen at all, being completely excluded, is irrefutable rejection.

Now, imagine that the team captain is God. It's one thing to be picked last for the third-grade kickball game, but it's another thing altogether to be "passed over," rejected by the eternal God of the universe. And instead of disappointment, embarrassment, and public humiliation, you've been taught that not being chosen means you're destined for eternity in hell.

Being chosen, we're told, is our assurance that we're accepted by the God we worship. If you're a Calvinist, you don't know why God chose you. You humbly assert that you only know that it's not because of who you are or anything you've ever done. If you're a non-Calvinist, you've been taught that God chose you because you chose him. Yet, you wonder how to reconcile this understanding with Jesus's words to his disciples, "You did not choose me, but I chose you" (John 15:16). But whether he chose us just because (Calvinism), or he chose us because we put our faith in Jesus (non-Calvinism), it doesn't really matter. Either way, we are chosen. God picked us. We are the elect. At least, that's what we're taught in many churches. But is that what the Bible teaches?

A Caution Against Christian Pride

In my story about our third-grade kickball team, what I didn't share with you was that even though I was never the last one picked, I was always jealous of a classmate named Sammy. Sammy was the best athlete in the school and was always the first to be chosen. Election/

choosing, by nature, is comparative. It always pits one person against another, the chosen against the unchosen. It forces a competing pool of people to compare their station with someone else. So when the pastor tells his congregation, "you all were chosen" (ignore for the moment the real probability that there are likely a good many non-Christians in the pews), we intuit that we are more special in some way than some others who were not chosen. In other words, being chosen by God gives us a certain satisfaction because it's confirmation that we're somehow, in some divine way, better, more worthy, wiser, or at least, more favored than someone else.

I once heard this very unflattering and convicting definition of pride (something detestable in the Scriptures): *pride is the pleasure we feel when we're better than someone else.* Jesus warns against this kind of spiritual snobbery when he tells his disciples not to be like the arrogant Pharisee who looked with disdain upon the lowly tax collector (Luke 18:10). The apostle Paul admonishes the elect in the church in Rome not to think of themselves more highly than they ought (Rom. 12:3), and he cautions the people of the church in Corinth not to be "puffed up in favor of one against another" (1 Cor. 4:6). This type of comparative and prideful mindset is exactly what C. S. Lewis refers to as "the complete anti-God state of mind."[12]

I believe that our desire to be special and liked and chosen and favored, our desire to elevate our stature in God's story, has caused us to muddle a foundational aspect of the biblical doctrine of election: it is not about us. By trying to squeeze ourselves into the first-century picture, we've corrupted the real message of an amazing plan enacted by God at the birth of the church—a plan that ensures that a maximum number of people will benefit from his gracious offer of eternal life. By carrying a first-century doctrine into the twenty-first century, we've turned the good news of the gospel into dreadful news for much of God's creation for most of Christian history. We've caused division in the body and tarnished the name "Christian" with the mortal sin of pride, pitting "us" against "them" by placing the contemptuous thought in people's minds that when it comes to salvation, everyone is either chosen or not chosen. The Calvinists are blunt in their message: God only chooses some of us. That's just the way it is. The traditional non-Calvinists try to soften the issue by the unsupportable, nonbiblical assertion that all Christians are chosen.

Neither position is biblical. Neither position is truth. So let's loose the chains. In the Bible, God has provided for us a freedom-producing, noncontradictory, true-to-Scripture, doctrine of election. Read on.

5

A NEW MODEL

So the word of the Lord continued to increase and prevail mightily. (Acts 19:20)

I began to read through the Bible with a renewed sense of purpose and with a goal of testing this new understanding of the doctrine of election against the pages of Scripture. With each reference to God's elect, it became more evident that "the elect" was not just another name for Christians or for the church but a special category of Christians, consisting of extraordinarily glorified individuals who were given a unique role in God's post-cross plan to save the world. In short, what I found was exactly what I had been seeking for more than a decade: a noncontradictory, true-to-Scripture understanding of the doctrine of election— the missing puzzle pieces. *The elect of the New Testament were individuals chosen by God from a single generation of people, divinely enabled to recognize the gospel as truth, and uniquely gifted to launch the church.*

A Really Good "Business" Model

In Chapter Two we saw where the Calvinistic model of the gospel failed to achieve the important goal of profitability, producing no increase for the kingdom. In the Calvinistic model, only those people who were chosen by God in some "secret counsel" from before the foundation of the world, got saved. Such a "gospel" offers only hopelessness, despair, and futility for the majority of God's creation—and it casts the gracious invitations by Jesus for "all to come" as insincere and disingenuous. Jesus's stated purpose of saving "the world" is completely absent from the Calvinistic model.

This new perspective on election and clear understanding of the role of the doctrine of election in God's plan to save the world through Jesus Christ, began to reveal a wonderful, new model of the gospel, one that ensures increase and guarantees profitability for God's soul-saving business. As expected, God's plan not only provides for kingdom growth, but also for the opportunity for everyone to respond, for all to be saved and come to the knowledge of the truth (1 Tim. 2:4). The model reveals God's sincere offer of good news for the whole world, not just a few "chosen" people.

Below is the new model that shows the outworking of God's biblical plan of salvation—a true-to-Scripture model of the gospel.

Father ➡ Apostles ➡ Jesus ➡ Apostles ➡ Elect ➡ Church ➡ World ➡ Father
                                    (glorified)   (glorified)

Here's how the model works:

- From before the foundation of the world, the Father chose twelve Jewish men—the apostles—to whom he supernaturally revealed Jesus as the Messiah (Matt. 16:17; Luke 8:10; John 1:49; 6:45, 69; Eph. 1:4).

- The Father gave the apostles to Jesus to train up as his replacements (John 6:37, 44, 65; 17:2, 6, 9; 18:9).

- Jesus sanctified the apostles (John 17:17–19) and glorified them with powerful gifting—the firstfruits of the Holy Spirit (John 20:22; Acts 1:8).

- Jesus sent the apostles to witness and proclaim the gospel message, but not to everyone indiscriminately. Their Spirit-led commission was to seek out a specific group of preappointed people who had been divinely enabled to receive their message. These are the elect (John 10:16; 17:20–22, Acts 13:48; 18:10; 2 Tim. 2:10).

- The elect were divinely gifted (glorified) and given the responsibility to continue the work of the apostles—persuading others of the truth of the gospel, kindling faith in unbelievers, and edifying new Christians (Eph. 4:11–12). Those who are convinced of the truth, and who repent and believe in Jesus, are the church.

- The church has a responsibility to grow in maturity, support each other, and to spread the gospel message to every tribe, tongue, people, and nation—that is, to the world.

- In the end, Jesus hands the kingdom—including all the world's faithful from all of redemptive history—back to the Father (John 14:6, 1 Cor. 15:24).

Those who do not repent and believe in Jesus as the Messiah, who do not take advantage of God's offer of saving grace and who refuse to love the truth, are justly condemned (Rom. 5:2; Eph. 2:8; 2 Thess. 2:10; Titus 2:11).

An Illustration

> *Oh that you would rend the heavens and come down, that the mountains might quake at your presence—as when fire kindles brushwood and the fire causes water to boil—to make your name known to your adversaries, and that the nations might tremble at your presence! (Isaiah 64:1-2)*

To illustrate the creative and effective strategy of this masterful "business plan," I thought of it much like the starting of a fire. In a way, God's goal was to set the world ablaze with a new religion called Christianity. With Jesus as the source, the fire itself, the apostles were like matches, sent to various regions to begin to set afire the kindling—the elect. Kindling, of course, is the material with special properties of combustibility, but it is only needed for a short time. The role of the elect was to set aflame the more enduring material, the firewood that continues to burn for long periods of time—the church. The church is to remain "burning" until "the coming of the day of God" (2 Pet. 3:12).

With Jesus as the cornerstone, God began constructing this new phase of his plan of salvation with three principal building blocks— the apostles, the elect, and the church.

The Apostles

> *Nathanael answered him, "Rabbi, you are the Son of God! You are the King of Israel!" (John 1:49)*

Before we can fully appreciate the role of the elect in the development of the church, it is important to understand the purpose and call of the apostles. I mentioned earlier that I don't believe the apostles are included in the elect as referenced by Jesus and by the writers of the New Testament. You might have noticed from my model of the gospel that the apostles are a separate and distinct entity from the elect. This is not to say that they weren't chosen by God; they definitely were. But they had a very unique role in God's plan to save the world.

I know that by separating the apostles from the entity in the New Testament writings referred to as "the elect," I am bucking traditional thinking and will likely cause some consternation for many. Yet I also know that one of the primary causes of contradictions in the various views of the doctrine of election occurs when we ignore the biblical uniqueness of each group and lump them together, treating them as a divinely chosen singularity.

Both the apostles and the elect were Christians. Both were examples of an unconditional election by God. Both were irresistibly called into service. Both were glorified with exceptional gifting, and both were part of the early church.. But I believe that the Bible clearly depicts the apostles and the elect as distinct entities, used by God to fulfill two distinct roles in the formation of the church.

While there are a number of differences that distinguish the apostles from the elect, one primary distinction is that, while the apostles were Jewish men drawn to the incarnate Jesus by the Father and divinely enabled to recognize him as the Messiah, the elect were made up of both Jews and Gentiles, men and women who were divinely chosen to receive the message of the apostles and supernaturally enabled to recognize the gospel as truth. Another way to understand this distinction is that the apostles were God-chosen, pre-cross Christian converts tasked to gather the elect, while the elect were God-chosen, post-cross converts, tasked to launch the church. Following are a few additional unique differences between the apostles and all other Christians, including the elect.

Taught by the Father

In one of the most amazing displays of divine providence, Jesus tells a very skeptical Nathanael that he (Jesus) saw him sometime earlier while Nathanael was sitting under a tree (John 1:43–51). This perplexing statement from Jesus seemed to strike at the very soul of Nathanael, causing him to suddenly blurt out, "You are the Son of God! You are the King of Israel!" What would cause such a surprising reaction and change of attitude from a man who, moments earlier, was grumbling to Philip that nothing good can come out of Nazareth (v. 46)?

Nathanael's reaction was a New Testament fulfillment of Isaiah's prophesy on display. "All your children shall be taught by the Lord" (Isa. 54:13). Jesus later told his followers, "Everyone who has heard and learned from the Father comes to me" (John 6:45). Nathanael had obviously experienced something supernatural while sitting under that tree—a teaching from the Father, perhaps a vision. While we're not told the exact nature of what Nathanael experienced, when Jesus tells him that he saw him, it's as if Nathanael, upon meeting Jesus in person, suddenly realized that what he experienced that day under the tree was the very presence of God, and that the cryptic message he received from the Father was now clear—this man, Jesus, was the Messiah.

This display of divine, supernatural enlightenment was unique to the apostles of Jesus Christ. The apostles had been chosen from before the foundation of the world, taught by the Father, drawn to Jesus, and divinely enabled to recognize Jesus as the Messiah. The special revelation to the apostles from the Father about the identity of Jesus is made clear for us in Matthew 16. After Jesus asks the apostles who people think that he is, Peter responds with a list that includes John the Baptist, Jeremiah, and Elijah—but no mention of

Jesus as the Christ, the long-awaited Messiah. Then, Jesus directs his gaze at Peter and asks,

> "But who do you say that I am?" Simon Peter replied, "You are the Christ, the Son of the living God." And Jesus answered him, "Blessed are you, Simon Bar-Jonah! For flesh and blood has not revealed this to you, but my Father who is in heaven." (Matt. 16:15–17)

Note that Jesus acknowledges that Peter was specifically "taught" by the Father that Jesus was the Christ. Of course, Jesus was thought to be many things by the general public—a good teacher, a prophet, a man who spoke with authority, a false witness, a bastard child—but only to the apostles did the Father reveal him to be the Messiah, the Son of the living God.

Apprentices

The twelve men, taught by the Father and chosen by Jesus, epitomized Paul's teaching to the church of Corinth that God chooses the weak, foolish, and unremarkable to carry out his world-saving plan, so that it may be evident that the glory is all God's, and no one may boast in themselves (1 Cor. 1:25–29). They had no applicable skill set for the task they were about to undertake. Yet, Jesus referred to this ragtag group as his "little flock" and his "little children." Later they will become his friends and ultimately, his brothers. For three years, day and night, Jesus taught, trained, prepared, equipped, and nurtured these men in a total-immersion apprenticeship program, encouraging, exhorting, and occasionally rebuking them. But for what purpose?

"If anyone would come after me, let him deny himself and take up his cross and follow me" (Matt. 16:24). With these words, spoken only to the Twelve, Jesus defined the true and unique purpose of apostleship. As Christians, we are "followers" of Jesus—disciples. But the phrase Jesus chooses, "come after," is not figurative. Unlike his use of the verb "follow" (Gr. *akoloutheō*) at the end of the passage, "come after" (Gr. *erchomai opisō*) is a reference to sequential order, not discipleship: first Jesus, then the apostles. Jesus was telling the Twelve that their calling was to take his place when he was gone. This verse makes clear the divine objective that, upon Jesus's death, the apostles were to be his replacements—not just his disciples. Jesus was teaching his "children" that they were to take over the business after his death. The Great Shepherd was training up other shepherds to care for his flock in his absence.

Shepherds

"But he who enters by the gate is the shepherd of the sheep.... I am the gate" (John 10:2, 9 NIV). In the tenth chapter of the Gospel of John, Jesus offers a stinging rebuke to the Pharisees. He calls them thieves and robbers because they gained *unauthorized* access to the sheep. They proclaimed themselves to be God's shepherds but did not enter the sheepfold through the gate. Only the true shepherds gain access through the gate. Jesus is the gate.

With this metaphor, Jesus was letting the leaders of Israel know that he would be sending the true shepherds (the apostles) into the world to call out their sheep, and only those given to Jesus by the Father (the gatekeeper, v. 3) would be given authorized access to the sheepfold. Note that while the apostles came to Jesus through the Father, those sheep who respond to their voice—those who receive their message—will follow the shepherds out of the sheepfold, through the gate (Jesus), to the Father (John 14:6). In other words, after the cross, "the gate" swings the other way. It is no longer a restricting barrier giving access only to the true shepherds but is now an open door of grace, allowing all who believe to leave the world and join the Father.

Glorified

At the end of the Gospel of Matthew, Jesus gives his eleven remaining apostles, the "Great Commission"—the task of making disciples of all nations (Matt. 28:19). This was no small undertaking for eleven completely unremarkable men living in one small corner of the world. But we soon realize that Jesus wasn't really sending mere men into the world. On the day of Pentecost, we witness a remarkably changed group of servants, men who had been visited by and glorified by the power of the Holy Spirit. They were no longer unremarkable, no longer weak, no longer foolish. They were now uniquely endowed with a full complement of divine powers at their disposal. Here are just three examples of their unique glorification.

1. *They were given the power to bind and to loose.* "I will give you the keys of the kingdom of heaven, and whatever you bind on earth shall be bound in heaven... and whatever you loose on earth shall be loosed in heaven" (Matt. 16:19, 18:18). While biblical scholars have different opinions as to exact nature of these powers of "binding" and "loosing" given to the apostles, what is undeniable is that, as the new representatives of God on earth, the actions and decisions made by the apostles would be completely in sync with the will of God. Imbued with the Holy Spirit, they were to be God's presence, God's voice, and God's arbiters in the world. Amazingly, this unparalleled authority given only to the apostles included the power to forgive sins, or to withhold forgiveness of sins (John 20:23).

2. *They received scriptural enlightenment.* In Luke 24, as the resurrected Jesus met with his apostles, we're told that Jesus opened their minds to understand the Scriptures (Luke 24:45). This divine enlightenment led the apostle Paul to tell the church of Corinth that the apostles have the very mind of Christ (1 Cor. 2:16). In the Gospel of Matthew, Jesus told the apostles not to worry about what they will say in their encounters as his ambassadors because they would be given the words to speak (Matt. 10:19). The early church fathers called the apostles the "guarantors of the tradition" because they were to ensure the accurate relaying of the truth exactly as taught by Jesus. These men were glorified with spiritual wisdom and insight into divine mysteries (1 Cor. 4:1), guided by the Spirit, and supernaturally reminded of all things taught to them by Jesus (John 14:26).

3. *They were given the firstfruits of the Holy Spirit.* When the apostle Paul referred to people who had "the firstfruits of the Spirit" (Rom. 8:23), I believe this was a reference to the supreme spiritual gifting of the apostles alone. We're told that these men were given "every spiritual blessing in the heavenly realm" (Eph. 1:3). They alone had the full complement of spiritual gifting. They raised the dead, gave sight to the blind, healed the lame, cast out demons, performed miracles, and had the unique power to impart spiritual gifts to others by the laying on of hands (Acts 19:6; Rom. 1:11).

The Apostolic Commission

These eleven shepherds were sent into the world as divinely glorified men—not mere mortals. And their commission was to use that glorification to "make disciples of all nations." But as mentioned, I propose that God's strategy was not to have them "shotgun" out the gospel message to everyone they encountered. Under the guidance of the Holy Spirit, these shepherds were to seek out a specific group of sheep. The apostles were messengers from God, sent into the world to gather together a predesignated group of people who had been divinely appointed to receive and respond to their message, a group called "the elect."

The Elect

> *Therefore I endure everything for the sake of the elect, that they also may obtain the salvation that is in Christ Jesus with eternal glory. (2 Timothy 2:10)*

The apostle Paul stormed out of the synagogue in the city of Corinth, frustrated with the local Jews who had become vocal and insulting in their opposition to his gospel message. "Your blood be on your own heads!" he cried in frustration and anger, as he resolved that from then on he would bring the good news only to the Gentiles (Acts 18:6). But one night soon thereafter, Jesus came to him in a vision and said, "I have many in this city who are my people" (vs. 10). So Paul continued for more than a year and a half to teach the word of God among the Corinthians, both Jews and Gentiles.

"My people," Jesus called them. And it is for the sake of these special people that Paul claimed the apostles were "being killed all the day long... [like] sheep to be slaughtered" (Rom. 8:36). Peter referred to them as people who were called to bless and to be blessed (1 Pet. 3:9). And the apostle John explained that these people received an anointing from the Spirit that "teaches you about everything" (1 John 2:27). These were the elect.

Just Christians?

In Chapter Three, I pointed out what I believe to be a common misunderstanding of Scripture; the fact that most current interpretations of the doctrine of election propose that all true Christians are considered to be the elect of God. And although they arrive at this conclusion from very different viewpoints, they all agree that "the elect" is just another name for true Christians, or for the church. However, I'm proposing that just as the apostles were not just disciples but a special subset of disciples, the elect were not just Christians but an incredibly unique subset of Christians.

My definition of God's elect makes four assertions that dispute the idea that "the elect" is just another name for all true Christians. I made the claim that the elect were:

1. of a single generation, contemporaries of the apostles,
2. chosen by God,
3. divinely enabled to receive the gospel, and
4. glorified with gifts by the Holy Spirit to be used to jumpstart the church.

While I readily acknowledge that there are always exceptions and that all things are possible with God, by contrast I believe that the typical, contemporary Christian:

1. is not of the New Testament elect,
2. was not chosen by God,
3. was not divinely enabled to receive the gospel, and
4. is not gifted with the same divine powers as the elect.

The apostle Paul gave us a key to understanding the distinctions between the elect and the typical Christian with these informative words from his final letter: "I endure everything for the sake of the elect" (2 Tim. 2:10). With those words, Paul seemed to be stating that his entire ministry had a single focus: the kindling and strengthening of the faith of a group called the elect. And he was not alone. Based on letters written by Peter and John, it seems that all the apostles were directing their outreach efforts to a predesignated group of people, the group Jesus referred to as "my people" (Acts 18:10), or as his "other sheep" (John 10:16). The commission of the apostles then, contrary to the belief of many, was not to proclaim the gospel indiscriminately to the world but to seek out a targeted group of people who had been divinely "teed up" to receive their message.

If we consider that everything Paul did and wrote was for the benefit of this specific group of people called "the elect," then when we read his letters in the New Testament, we can gather a pretty clear understanding of who these people were. According to the apostle, the elect were: sanctified in Christ, called to be saints (1 Cor. 1:2); loved by God (Rom. 1:7); marked with the seal of the Holy Spirit (Eph. 1:13); granted belief (Phil. 1:29); and reconciled to God (Col. 1:22). Yet they also had natural limitations (Rom. 6:19) as people of the flesh—infants in Christ (1 Cor. 3:1). They were deserting him who called them, turning to a different gospel (Gal. 1:6) and departing from the faith (1 Tim. 4:1).

Admittedly in many ways this group, the elect, sounds a lot like typical Christians in any evangelical church today—blessed in many wonderful ways, yet struggling to grow and persevere in the faith. But upon further examination of the New Testament letters we see some important differences—unique qualities that distinguish the elect from the typical Christian and from the church as a whole. Let's look at those differences now.

Unique

1. The elect were divinely enabled to receive the gospel as truth. The gospel story defies credibility. We read over and over in our Bibles about complete pagans who, upon hearing a single presentation of the gospel, cast off all skepticism, ignore all scorn, expose themselves to persecution—even torture and death—and yet they believe this completely irrational story about God who became man, walked on water, controlled the weather, was despised by his own people, crucified, buried, came back to life, and floated up to heaven. And, oh yeah, belief in this crazy story is the only way they could avoid eternal torture in a place called "the lake of fire." Yet, some people immediately responded positively to this completely improbable gospel message delivered by completely improbable messengers. How could this be?

In a spiritual sense, the task of the apostles was to bring dead people back to life. In the New Testament writings we witness a supernatural spiritual "quickening" of select people. The telling of the gospel, the good news about Jesus Christ, seemed to be the spark of life in some, but not all, of these "dead souls." We see in Acts 2:41 that three thousand were added to the number of believers. That's a great many, but not all who were present in Jerusalem for the festivities at Pentecost. In Acts 5:14, "multitudes" were added. In Acts 11:24, "a great many" were added. In Acts 13:48, "as many as were appointed to eternal life believed." While the number of people who responded to the gospel and became new believers was significant, it was far from everyone. It seems that only those who were divinely enabled, predisposed, appointed, and ordained to receive the gospel believed.

At this point, the Calvinist would nod in agreement that this is the expected response of those who were chosen by God. They would suggest that this positive response of so many people to the gospel message is evidence of an irresistible grace, an "internal call," given only to the elect. And I agree. Yet the conversion of so many after just a *single* telling of the gospel represents a huge disparity between what we read in the book of Acts at the onset of the church and what we experience today in evangelical Christianity. Something very unique was happening in the initial days of the early church.

I remember reading years ago that the average believer had heard some form of the gospel seventeen times before responding with belief. When I think of my own journey of faith, that number sounds about right. As a toddler, my mother used to read Bible stories out of a big yellow children's book—the gospel. Throughout my grade-school years, I attended Sunday school classes—the gospel. In junior high school, my friends and I got "caught" a number of times by the "God Squad" (Campus Crusade for Christ) at the beach—the gospel. In high school I attended a Young Life program (one time)—the gospel. And in college I was approached on several occasions by a Christian club—the gospel. I'm sure I heard the gospel dozens of times, yet it wasn't until I was in my thirties that the message took root. And even then, it began as just a spark. It took several additional years to really develop into a true Christian faith.

This is not to say that there aren't some people today who, upon hearing the gospel for the first time, respond positively and place their trust in Jesus. It is not even to say that God doesn't ever suddenly, supernaturally quicken someone's heart through dreams and visions, revealing Jesus as Lord and Savior. I'm saying that what we see in the early church is not the *typical* response of unbelievers to the gospel message. In the writings of the New Testament, we witness the supernatural phenomenon of the effect of the gospel on those who had been divinely predisposed to receive it as truth—the elect.

2. The elect were glorified with powerful spiritual gifts. Just as the apostles were appointed to replace Jesus after his departure, the elect were appointed to "come after" the apostles. And just as the apostles were glorified with the "firstfruits of the Spirit" (Rom. 8:23) to help them in their commission to kindle the faith of the elect, the elect were also glorified with unique and powerful spiritual gifts to be used to continue the work of the apostles in launching the church.

When the apostle Paul wrote, "For we know, brothers loved by God, that he has chosen you, because our gospel came to you not only in word, but also in power and in the Holy Spirit and with full conviction" (1 Thess. 1:4–5), he was acknowledging that the supernatural power received by these believers in the church at Thessalonica upon receiving the gospel was evidence that they were among those chosen by God. Many seemed to receive spiritual gifting upon conversion, while others received spiritual gifts in a subsequent act of grace through the laying on of hands by the apostles. But regardless of how the elect were enabled, I believe that the purpose of their gifting was to give them credibility as true vessels of God, to help them kindle faith in unbelievers, to strengthen the faith of believers, and to manage the affairs of the fledgling Church.

While all of the lists of spiritual gifts in the Bible are descriptions of God's supernatural grace, in my opinion the gifting of the elect is summarized in Hebrews 6. The writer of Hebrews tells us that the elect were "enlightened... tasted the heavenly gift... shared in the Holy Spirit... tasted the goodness of the word of God and the powers of the age to come" (Heb. 6:4–5). Although many scholars want to spin this passage to downplay the powerful gifts described and the consequences (or even the possibility) of apostasy of the elect, what we read in this passage is an inventory of a far superior level of gifting than experienced by the average Christian. It is a description of divine glorification.

The writer goes on to remind his elect readers that with this special empowerment comes a high standard of accountability. As with all blessings from God, these amazing gifts came with a great responsibility to serve God and to use them for the intended purpose. According to the writer of Hebrews, if the elect were to ever fall away, due to their unique position as trustees of God's redemptive plan for the world and as God's chosen role models to the new covenant community, there would be no hope of restoring them to repentance, since they would be "crucifying once again the Son of God to their own harm and holding him up to contempt" (Heb. 6:6). The implication is that the potential damage to God's world-saving purpose caused by the snubbing of God's grace and the ultimate rejection of the faith by his elect servants, would be such that it would render the apostasy of the elect uniquely unforgiveable.

3. The elect were chosen by God as the "firstfruits" to be saved. Declaring that the elect were chosen by God is generally accepted by all Christians, since the very meaning of the word "elect" is "chosen." However, the apostle Paul tells the elect in Thessalonica, "God chose you as the firstfruits to be saved" (2 Thess. 2:13). The word "firstfruits" (or "from the beginning," Gr. *apo archē*) implies that the people being addressed were the initial people to receive the salvific grace of the gospel, "the power of God for salvation" (Rom. 1:16). It would be hard to defend the notion that such a description could be applied to new believers even a generation later, and a meaningless anachronism in reference to modern-day Christians.

James uses similar language in his epistle to the twelve tribes of the dispersion. "Of his own will he brought us forth by the word of truth, that we should be a kind of firstfruits of his creatures" (Jas. 1:18). If we consider that, from a spiritual perspective, when Jesus died on the cross everyone died (2 Cor. 5:14), the reference by James that the elect were the "firstfruits of his creatures" becomes clear. The Christian is seen by God to be a new species of human being, a new creation (2 Cor. 5:17), The elect were chosen to be the first to be "awakened" by the message of the apostles and to receive new life.

We see a final reference to the firstfruits of God's new creation in the book of Revelation, when the apostle John sees a vision of people who "have been redeemed from mankind as firstfruits for God and the Lamb, and in their mouth no lie was found, for they are blameless" (Rev. 14:4–5). I believe that in this passage, John received a heavenly vision of those of the elect who remained faithful to their special calling and were experiencing the reward of eternal fellowship with God.

In summation, the elect of the New Testament were an integral part of a unique church-development strategy—a one-time tactic employed by God at the initial launching of the church.

A Single Generation

Truly, I say to you, all these things will come upon this generation. (Matthew 23:36)

I doubt that my definition of the elect as people chosen, enabled, or gifted by God is going to be especially controversial to anyone who believes that the doctrine of election is biblical. But my belief that the New Testament elect were of a single generation, contemporary with the apostles, is likely to cause some heartburn among those who subscribe to the understanding that "the elect" is just another name for true Christians. They would likely argue that there is no warrant to restrict the decree of New Testament election to a single generation.

I disagree. By trying to force a uniquely first-century work of God to initiate the early church, into a universally applicable doctrine for all Christians for all time, theologians have created "tension" where none is warranted. However, as soon as we properly restrict the elect to a single generation, the various texts that seemed so paradoxical suddenly become clear and obvious. Here is a brief defense of the assertion that the elect were, in a manner of speaking, the *original* greatest generation.

A Familiar Pattern

It would not be without precedent for God to choose to work in a special way with a select group of people from a single generation as he launches a new plan for his people. For example, as God was establishing the nation of Israel, his first "chosen" people, note that four of the first five books of the Bible are focused on a single generation of Israelites. In these books—Exodus, Leviticus, Numbers, Deuteronomy—we read where, even though everyone in the newly forming nation of Israel received the unique blessings and privileges of being God's special people, within the community were some particular individuals, chosen by God and divinely enabled to conduct business on his behalf. The anointing of the leaders, the formation of the priesthood, and the gifting of tabernacle craftsman were just a few of the many divine callings to ensure that this new venture would progress as designed. These divinely anointed individuals were the chosen core through whom God would begin to realize his plan for the world.

In the New Testament, God was launching a new plan but with a familiar pattern of grace. The anointing of the leaders, the formation of the priesthood, and the gifting of those who were constructing the new tabernacle—the church—is a recognizable model. Similar to the formation and inauguration of the nation of Israel, God chose some people out of the world to use in a special way. When Peter told the early Christians, the "elect exiles of the dispersion" (1 Pet. 1:1), that they were a "chosen generation" (1 Pet. 2:9), he was acknowledging a particular working by God in these people. He went on to state that it was God's calling that brought them out of darkness—a reference to the divine enablement and act of grace that allowed some individuals from this special generation to respond to the gospel with unique receptivity.

The Time Is Near

It is evident that the writers of the New Testament did not foresee that the church age would endure beyond their own generation. In fact, it is clear from their writings that they believed that the prophesied second coming of Jesus would happen in their lifetime. When the apostle Paul told the church in Rome, "The God of peace will soon crush Satan under your feet" (Rom. 16:20), the readers would likely have assumed that "your feet" referred to themselves—their generation—and that "soon" meant imminently. It is likely that neither Paul nor the Christians in Rome would have understood that the "you" was transcendent, and that the actual crushing of Satan would not occur for thousands of years.

This is only one example of many that provides evidence that the general belief of the early church was that "the time is near," and that God was initiating his plan through the elect "at the present time," and that all of the predictive prophesies regarding the end of the church age and the second coming of Christ would occur "soon" and during "this generation." In other words, the writers of the New Testament letters were not writing with us (or any future generation) in mind at all. The fact that we can find valuable application and wise counsel for today's church in much of what they wrote is a testimony to the divine work of the Holy Spirit, but future applications of their message was not in the minds of the writers nor of their first-century readers.

Firstfuits

Previously, I cited three references from Scripture where people were referred to as "firstfruits." The apostle Paul told the Thessalonians that they were "the firstfruits to be saved" (2 Thess. 2:13). James told his readers that they were "the firstfruits of his creatures" (Jas. 1:18). And the apostle John saw a vision of people in heaven described as "the firstfruits for God and the Lamb" (Rev. 14:4). Most scholars believe both Paul's letter to the Thessalonians and the letter from James were written about the year AD 50. It is not likely that we, the Christian community two thousand years later—or even any subsequent generation after the writing of those letters—would be considered "firstfruits to be saved" or the "firstfruits of his creatures." These references only become confusing or paradoxical when we take them out of their first-century context and try to apply them to future generations.

Trans-covenantal Saints

The writer of the book of Hebrews seems to allude to a special provision of grace and redemption for a group of people whose lives spanned the transition between the phasing out of the old covenant and the ushering in of the new covenant:

> Therefore he is the mediator of a new covenant, so that those who are called may receive the promised eternal inheritance, since a death has occurred that redeems them from the transgressions committed under the first covenant. (Heb. 9:15)

As indicated in an earlier chapter, "those who are called" is a synonym for the elect—people summoned into service by God. And the reference to redemption from "transgressions committed under the first covenant" clearly eliminates the possibility that the writer, in addressing "the called," could be including any generation beyond those who were alive prior to the full induction of the new covenant. Only people living concurrent with the apostles' generation could have had sins to their account which were committed under the first covenant.

Finally, when we consider that the whole purpose of the divine enabling of the elect was to continue the work begun by the apostles, ensuring the successful launching of the early church, and that we, the contemporary Christian church, are witnesses to the success of the efforts of these faithful first-century saints, the need for additional generations of equally glorified individuals—additional "elect" people—doesn't seem necessary. I believe that while both the apostles and the elect are examples of unconditional election and irresistible grace, God has always desired that his disciples choose to love and obey him freely—not because he determinedly overrode our free will, but because he revealed his majesty and beauty to the world, and because he first loved us.

The Church

> *What determines our brotherhood is what that man is by reason of Christ. Our community with one another consists solely in what Christ has done to both of us. This is true not merely at the beginning, as though in the course of time something else were to be added to our community; it remains so for all the future and to all eternity.*
>
> —*Dietrich Bonhoeffer*

On the cross, Jesus was drawing the world—the entire mass of sinful humanity—to himself (John 12:32). And according to the Scriptures, when Jesus died, *everyone* died (2 Cor. 5:14). This means that when Jesus first arose and emerged from the tomb as the "firstborn from the dead" (Col. 1:18), the "firstborn of all creation" (Col. 1:15), he stepped out into a spiritually dark, desolate world filled with "dead" people. Yet, when the risen Jesus appeared, it was like the first ray of sunlight in the morning, peeking over the horizon, casting its light and illuminating the bleak spiritual landscape. The darkness began to retreat. Light, life, and warmth were on the way. The night was over. A new hope was born.

Mary Magdalene encountered the risen Lord in the garden surrounding the tomb. In her spiritual deadness, she didn't recognize him. But in Jesus was life, and his life-giving gospel message to her was simple. "Mary," he said softly, barely above a whisper. That's it—the still small voice of God. The Good Shepherd called his sheep by name and at that moment, her spiritual eyes opened to see Jesus as Lord. She was born again—effectively, the "second-born" from the dead and the first to experience the new hope. We could rightfully say that Mary Magdalene was the first member of the Christian Church.

Jesus told her, "Go tell my brothers," and Mary ran to share the gospel with the apostles, the good news that Jesus had risen. Later that day, the Life-giver "awakened" his apostles, instructing them to go into the world and begin the work of quickening dead souls, starting with the elect, those who had been divinely prepared to receive the message, divinely gifted to share the message, and uniquely appointed to begin the work of building the Church upon their foundation.

Nonelect Christians

Although the elect were predisposed to receive the gospel message, it is not my belief that the elect were the only people who were able to respond to the apostolic presentations of the gospel. There were many others who, upon hearing the words of the apostles and the subsequent teachings of the divinely gifted elect, were drawn by the now-present Holy Spirit to the truth of the message, "For the grace of God has appeared that offers salvation to all people" (Titus 2:11, NIV). After the cross, Jesus unleashed the Holy Spirit into the world and swung the door of God's saving grace wide open so that "whosoever" could believe and could share in the blessings as part of the body of Christ, the church.

In his first letter to the Corinthians, the apostle Paul spoke of "outsiders" and "unbelievers" coming into the church, hearing God's word, being convicted, and worshipping God (1 Cor. 14:24–25). Some scholars believe that the implication of the term "outsiders" is that these people were not spiritually gifted, which would distinguish them from the elect in the local congregation. I believe that Paul acknowledged these new nonelect believers in his letter to the church in Corinth when he wrote:

> To the church of God in Corinth, to those sanctified in Christ Jesus and called to be his holy people, together with all those everywhere who call on the name of our Lord Jesus Christ—their Lord and ours (1 Cor. 1:2, NIV).

The church then, at its onset, was made up of two categories of believers. One group was comprised of those "sanctified in Christ Jesus and called." The apostles and the elect were part of this group, unconditionally and monergistically chosen by God and irresistibly recruited into kingdom service. We could say these people were chosen in a very Calvinistic manner. In the other group were those "who call on the name of the Lord Jesus Christ." These were the nonelect believers. They became part of the church because, thanks to the grace of God and the convicting power of the Holy Spirit, they responded to the gospel, calling on the name of the Lord. Three times in Scripture we're told that "*anyone* who calls on the name of the Lord will be saved" (Joel 2:32; Acts 2:21; Rom. 10:13). We could say that these people were converted in a very non-Calvinistic manner—not irresistibly drawn, but freely choosing to submit to the lordship of Jesus and accepting the gracious offer of salvation. Paul seemed to go out of his way to make clear that both groups, the elect and the nonelect Christians, were worshipping the same God.

Scripture tells us that, ultimately, the manner in which both the elect and the nonelect become Christians is not by divine fiat but by the power of the gospel. When the apostle Paul wrote that "the gospel... is the power of God for salvation to everyone who believes" (Rom. 1:16), he was explaining the divine salvific power of the gospel and the universal process by which people typically become part of the church. This process is more clearly detailed in Paul's letter to the Ephesians.

> In him you also, when you heard the word of truth, the gospel of your salvation, and believed in him, were sealed with the promised Holy Spirit, who is the guarantee of our inheritance until we acquire possession of it, to the praise of his glory. (Eph. 1:13–14)

Hearing of the gospel—the word of truth, believing in Jesus, and receiving the Holy Spirit—that's the normative sequence available to everyone. It is the *ordo salutis*—the process which gives "whosoever will" access to the amazing power of God described throughout the New Testament simply as grace.

As a final note, even though it is nonelect believers who make up the body of today's church, this is not to say that God no longer calls people into kingdom service. Quite the contrary. Through the ministry of the Holy Spirit, God is still building his church through his divine call on the hearts of believers and through their reflection of his grace to others.

6

YEAH, BUT WHAT ABOUT...?

but test everything; hold fast what is good.
(1 Thessalonians 5:21)

There are several credible reports about a time when the irascible W. C. Fields, the crotchety old comedian from the 1940s, was found sitting in the garden with an open Bible and a martini. When asked, "What are you doing?," his reply was simply, "Looking for loopholes."

For the next five years in my journey to discover a noncontradictory, true-to-Scripture interpretation of the doctrine of election, I sought to put my new understanding to the test. Like W. C. Fields, I searched the Scriptures for loopholes—cracks, weaknesses, counterarguments—to my new, burden-lifting understanding that the doctrine of election as presented in the New Testament was simply a first-century strategy implemented by God to help get the early church up and running, and that it had no direct application for contemporary Christians.

God encourages us to reason, discern, be wise, use our minds, and test all things. With everything we read and hear regarding spiritual things, we are to be testing them against the word of God, keeping what is true and discarding that which is error. Although my search for loopholes involved the rereading of many commentaries, the relistening to many discussions, the reviewing of many debates, and the revisiting of nearly all my resources on the topic of election and predestination, the main source of scrutiny and focus was the Bible itself.

Before we turn to the Scriptures, we should acknowledge the fact that in a debate that has simmered for centuries with no resolve, we're not apt to find any completely unarguable evidence supporting one perspective or another—no sudden "aha" moments. The clues are likely going to be subtle and nuanced. Our challenge is to approach the passages from a clear and unbiased viewpoint. We need to be courageous enough to untether ourselves from all presuppositions and come to the word of God as Nicodemus came to Jesus—like an inquisitive child seeking the truth.

In this chapter, I wanted to anticipate some possible arguments to ensure that my understanding would withstand any opposition from Reformed and non-Calvinist objectors. Since nearly all traditional thinking regarding New Testament election posits that all true Christians are the elect of God, I've selected three amazing, yet provocative passages of Scripture that are commonly cited in reference to the doctrine of election and predestination, but which I believe are mistakenly interpreted as normative, that is, misapplied to all Christians for all time: Ephesians 1:3–14, Romans 8:28–30, and Romans 9:21–23. To be clear, it is not my intention to offer an exhaustive exegesis of these texts but to briefly show that, while normative interpretations miss the mark, these profound, awe-inspiring passages still provide wonderful applications for today's nonelect Christian.

Ephesians 1:3–14

³*Blessed be the God and Father of our Lord Jesus Christ, who has blessed us in Christ with every spiritual blessing in the heavenly places,*

⁴*even as he chose us in him before the foundation of the world, that we should be holy and blameless before him. In love*

⁵*he predestined us for adoption to himself as sons through Jesus Christ, according to the purpose of his will,*

⁶*to the praise of his glorious grace, with which he has blessed us in the Beloved.*

⁷*In him we have redemption through his blood, the forgiveness of our trespasses, according to the riches of his grace,*

⁸*which he lavished upon us, in all wisdom and insight*

⁹*making known to us the mystery of his will, according to his purpose, which he set forth in Christ*

¹⁰*as a plan for the fullness of time, to unite all things in him, things in heaven and things on earth.*

¹¹*In him we have obtained an inheritance, having been predestined according to the purpose of him who works all things according to the counsel of his will*

¹²*so that we who were the first to hope in Christ might be to the praise of his glory.*

¹³*In him you also, when you heard the word of truth, the gospel of your salvation, and believed in him, were sealed with the promised Holy Spirit,*

¹⁴*who is the guarantee of our inheritance until we acquire possession of it, to the praise of his glory.*

Question: Don't these verses say that all true Christians were chosen from before the foundation of the world and predestined to believe in Jesus?

Answer: No, and no.

According to this passage, those who were chosen from before the foundation of the world (v. 4), predestined for adoption (v. 5), blessed in the Beloved (v. 6), redeemed and forgiven (v. 7), and lavished with wisdom and insight into the mystery of God's will (vv. 8–9) are those who were "the first to hope in Christ" (v. 12). While some of the blessings described in the passage certainly apply to all Christians, Paul's intent in this opening statement to the church in Ephesus was not to extol the blessings of all Christians but to underline his own standing and authority as an apostle of Jesus Christ. The phrase "those who were the first to hope in Christ" eliminates any speculation that Paul is making a universal statement intended to include all Christians for all time. Furthermore, since this letter was likely written twenty-five to thirty years after Jesus's death, it seems improbable that Paul would consider the elect saints in Ephesus to be part of those who were "the first to hope in Christ" either, since there were likely many thousands of believers spanning two generations by this time in the history of the early church.

A further indication that Paul did not consider his readers in Ephesus to be part of the group he references in verses 3 through 12 is Paul's pivotal phrase in verse 13:

> *And you also* were included in Christ when you heard the message of truth, the gospel of your salvation. When you believed, you were marked in him with a seal, the promised Holy Spirit. (Eph. 1:13, emphasis added)

With those words, Paul turns his attention to his target audience, the elect in Ephesus, and begins to include them, but in *contrast* to the previous statements. In verses 3 through 12, "*we*" were chosen, blessed, redeemed, forgiven, and graced. In verses 13–14, "*you also*" were marked with the seal of the Holy Spirit when "*you* [all]... heard the gospel... and believed." Paul is drawing a contrast between the authority given to the apostles and blessings given to the Ephesian elect. Paul went on to pray that they too, would receive wisdom and revelation (Eph. 1:17), gifts of grace already obtained by the "we" in the passage (vv. 8–9). And in Chapter 3, Paul clarifies that these gifts (wisdom and revelation) were uniquely given to the "holy apostles and prophets" (Eph. 3:5).

Many of Paul's letters reveal that, because of his former reputation as a persecutor of Christians, he often had to justify his apostleship to the various churches. I believe that in Ephesians 1:3–12 Paul was offering a brief apostolic resumé—a recounting of apostolic gifting, and a confirmation of the divine appointment of the apostles—in part to establish his credibility as God's ambassador to the Ephesian elect. The "we," "us," and "our" are references to the apostles of Jesus Christ. Those described as chosen from before the foundation of the world and predestined do not include the elect or the future church.

Here is my paraphrase of Ephesians 1:3–14:

> We are the apostles, chosen from before the foundation
> of the world and predestined to be supremely glorified
> in Christ. You are the elect. You, too, have been blessed
> by God.

The Good News for All Christians

Paul begins this section of Scripture with the universal key to being blessed by God—being "in Christ." Those who are *in Christ* are not under condemnation (Rom. 8:1). Paul tells us that "if *anyone* is in Christ, he is a new creation" (2 Cor. 5:17, emphasis added), and those *in Christ* are God's "children, through faith" (Gal. 3:26). We're told that faith, love, grace, and purpose are *in Christ* (1 Tim. 1:14; 2 Tim. 1:9); and that the appropriate Christian mindset of humility is ours *in Christ* (Phil. 2:3–5).

One source of much confusion with the proper interpretation of this passage of Scripture is the fact that so many of the apostolic blessings Paul describes in the passage are also available to all who are "in Christ." We who are "in Christ" have also been redeemed by his blood (v. 7), forgiven of our trespasses (v. 7), and sealed with the Holy Spirit (v. 13). As Christians, we celebrate the fact that the corpus of New Testament writings makes it clear that these are all wonderful blessings to be cherished and enjoyed by all believers.

Romans 8:28–30

> ²⁸*And we know that for those who love God all things work together for good, for those who are called according to his purpose.*
>
> ²⁹*For those whom he foreknew he also predestined to be conformed to the image of his Son, in order that he might be the firstborn among many brothers.*
>
> ³⁰*And those whom he predestined he also called, and those whom he called he also justified, and those whom he justified he also glorified.*

Question: Doesn't this passage say that God foreknew all Christians and predestined us to heaven?

Answer: No, and no.

To understand these verses in their proper context we have to go back to verse 23:

> And not only the creation, but we ourselves, who have the firstfruits of the Spirit, groan inwardly as we wait eagerly for adoption as sons, the redemption of our bodies.

It is at this point in the letter that Paul begins to address the grace uniquely given to the apostles. The expression "we ourselves" in Scripture is often used to make an emphatic distinction between the writer and the readers (2 Thess. 1:4, 2 Pet. 1:18). Paul is stating that "we ourselves" (the apostles), and not "you" (the elect in Rome), were given the "firstfruits of the Spirit." The implication is that the apostles were not only the first to receive the Holy Spirit, but were given the complete complement of all the spiritual gifts of grace and an exclusive enduement of divine powers which included raising the dead, healing the lame, restoring the sick, prophesying, imparting spiritual gifts, etc. Having been filled with the Spirit of Christ (Acts 2:4), they were in complete sync with the will of God. Although Paul's readers, the elect in Rome, were also experiencing some divine spiritual gifting, they did not have the same powers or the same authority given to the apostles by Jesus.

There has been much interpretive focus placed on verses 29–30, traditionally referred to as "the golden chain of redemption" by both Calvinists and non-Calvinists. The traditional interpretation of this passage hinges on the understanding that Paul is detailing a sequence of God-ordained events for the salvation of true Christians that climaxes in a state of eternal glorification of the believer. It assumes that the glorification Paul is referring to at the end of the chain is the final disposition of the believer, involving his ultimate spiritual standing in the kingdom after his temporal death, including the acquisition of a redeemed and glorified body.

I don't consider this passage to be about redemption at all, nor do I believe that it can be universally applied to all Christians. In this passage, Paul is describing the divine sequence by which the apostles were foreknown (fore-chosen) by God from time in eternity past (Eph. 1:4), predestined to the divine office of apostle (Rom. 8:29), called into service at the God-determined time (Matt. 10:1-4, Rom. 1:1), justified through a unique act of consecration by Jesus (John 17:19), and glorified (divinely empowered) with the firstfruits of the Spirit (Rom. 8:23). I believe that Romans 8:29–30 would more appropriately be called "the golden chain of apostolic glorification."

The common misinterpretation of this passage begins with a misunderstanding of Paul's use of the word "glorified" (Gr. *doxazō*). Would a person not be considered to be glorified if he were:

- consecrated/sanctified by Jesus (John 17:19)?
- given the keys to the kingdom of heaven (Matt. 16:19)?
- supernaturally enlightened to understand the Scriptures (Luke 24:45)?
- given the power to raise the dead (Acts 9:40)?
- given the authority to forgive sin or to withhold forgiveness of sin (John 20:23)?

Without argument, such a person would be amazingly glorified. These are all descriptors of the powers and enablement given to the apostles. If we allow that the term "glorified" in Romans 8:30 is not referring to the final state that occurs after the death of the believer, but to the divine gifting and enablement given specifically to Paul and the other apostles, then the traditional interpretation that the verse describes a normative process of salvation completely unravels—and with it, all of the doctrinal conflicts imposed upon the verse, including the excruciating difficulty of understanding and explaining Paul's use of past-tense (aorist) verbs.

Here is my paraphrase of Romans 8:28–30:

> God blesses those who obey him. God is faithful. After all, look what an amazing divine work he has done in us, his apostles!

The Good News for All Christians

When Paul begins a sentence with "And we know" (v. 28), he is about to express something that has been commonly observed in the past or something that should be evident to all from the Old Testament Scriptures (v. 22). Here, Paul is saying that God is *notorious* for blessing those who love/obey (1 John 5:3) him. This has been God's pattern. Implied in verse 28 is the faithfulness of God to continue to work things out for the benefit of those who are faithful to him. When the people in Capernaum asked Jesus what God required of them, Jesus' simple response was "believe in him whom he has sent" (John 6:28–29). God's blessings are still available to all who believe in Jesus.

Additionally, in contrast to the exclusive phrase "we ourselves" in verse 23 is the inclusive phrase "us all" in verse 32.

> He who did not spare his own Son but gave him up for us all, how will he not also with him graciously give us all things?

With this verse Paul momentarily invites the readers back into the blessings—specifically, the atoning work on the cross. Whenever Paul uses the expression "we all" or "us all" he is assuring us that what follows can be applied to all Christians (Rom. 4:16, 2 Cor.

3:18, Eph. 2:3). In this case, it's the reminder that the atonement achieved on the cross was an offer of redemption open to all. The apostle John echoes this wonderful affirmation regarding the universal effect of the cross when he says, "He is the propitiation for our sins, and not for ours only but also for the sins of the whole world" (1 John 2:2). As Christians, we can rejoice in the understanding that Jesus's death on the cross opened the door of saving grace for everyone, without exception.

Romans 9:21–23

> [21]Has the potter no right over the clay, to make out of the same lump one vessel for honorable use and another for dishonorable use?
>
> [22]What if God, desiring to show his wrath and to make known his power, has endured with much patience vessels of wrath prepared for destruction,
>
> [23]in order to make known the riches of his glory for vessels of mercy, which he has prepared beforehand for glory...

Question: Doesn't this passage say that God predetermined some people to be saved and others to go to hell?

Answer: No, and no.

An unbiased reading of this verse clearly refutes the Reformed position that, from the beginning of time and for reasons unrevealed, God has divided everyone into two groups—those he predestined for heaven and those he predestined for hell. Paul makes special note that the potter begins his work with *a single lump of clay*, not two different lumps. This is consistent with his earlier discussion in the same chapter regarding Jacob and Esau (vv. 10–13). The fact that they were twins, "conceived by one man" (v. 10), reinforces their single-source generation, assuring us that God does not create people from two different and distinct lumps of clay—one lump of "good/honorable" material and another of "defective/dishonorable" material. As some well-known and wise men once said, "We hold these truths to be self-evident, that all men are created equal"—and are formed by the same just and loving God, with no predetermined final eternal disposition.

What's in view in this passage is how God, the potter, shapes/molds/crafts the individual based on the person's heart of devotion to God and obedience to his commands. The Bible tells us that God is a searcher of hearts (Rom. 8:27, Jer. 17:10, Ps. 129:23), and is looking for those whose hearts are fully committed to him (2 Chron. 16:9). Why would God need to search anyone's heart if their fate had been predetermined? This vessel-shaping of God is unmistakably reinforced in Jeremiah 18:5–10 and 2 Timothy 2:21, where the molding of the vessel (honorable or dishonorable/common) is a reaction to the behaviors of the person (or the nation).

> Then the word of the Lord came to me: "O house of Israel, can I not do with you as this potter has done? declares the Lord. Behold, like the clay in the potter's hand, so are you in my hand, O house of Israel. If at any time I declare concerning a nation or a kingdom, that I will pluck up and break down and destroy it, and if that nation, concerning which I have spoken, turns from its evil, I will relent of the disaster that I intended to do to it. And if at any time I declare concerning a nation or a kingdom that I will build and plant it, and if it does evil

in my sight, not listening to my voice, then I will relent of the good that I had intended to do to it." (Jer. 18:5–10)

Therefore, if anyone cleanses himself from what is dishonorable, he will be a vessel for honorable use, set apart as holy, useful to the master of the house, ready for every good work. (2 Tim. 2:21)

Note that a person's (or a nation's) own actions determine the divine "shaping" of the person (or nation). Furthermore, in both of these passages is the clear teaching that the decree by God is not necessarily permanent. If a person "cleanses himself" or if a nation "turns from its evil," God will "reshape" that vessel accordingly.

In verses 22 and 23, remembering that Paul is responding to the hypothetical question, "Is there injustice on God's part?" (v. 20), Paul's answer seems to be; "Would you still think God was unjust if you knew that throughout history, God, although prepared and justly intending to destroy disobedient & unfaithful people (vessels of wrath prepared for destruction), *instead*, chose to endure them with patience in order to more effectively display his glory to those people he has sovereignly chosen (vessels of mercy) to divinely enable (glorify) to carry out his purposes?"

These verses were an obvious reference to the familiar event in Exodus 32 where God's servant Moses (his vessel of mercy prepared beforehand, predestined for glory) interceded for the rebellious, idolatrous people of Israel (vessels of wrath prepared/destined for destruction), invoking God's ire and desire to destroy them. God relented because, in his wisdom, he knew that in the eyes of his servant Moses, his glory would be more greatly and effectively displayed by grace, compassion, and mercy than by wrath, power, and destruction.

Here's my paraphrase of Romans 9:21–23:

God is good. God is just. Heaven or hell is up to us.

The Good News for All Christians

In these verses, as sinners, we are the "vessels of wrath prepared for destruction." We are not the "vessels of mercy chosen beforehand for glory." Our just God has two choices to deal with sinners: destroy them as they deserve; or show mercy, waiting with patience for their decision with regard to his Son. Both actions would display his glory but God, in his love, has determined that not only are mercy and compassion more powerful displays of glory than wrath and destruction, but by manifesting his grace God has given us the model by which we are to reflect these same attributes—mercy and compassion—to others. Through his willingness to show mercy over wrath, God has demonstrated for us the amazing power of forgiveness over bitterness; kindness over cruelty; gentleness over brutishness. When we display these attributes to others as a natural outflow of God's grace, it reveals that we truly understand and cherish the immeasurable grace that God has shown to us.

7

REVERBERATIONS

Unless the Lord builds the house, those who build it labor in vain.

(Psalm 127:1)

In any construction project, the integrity of the work of each trade is dependent upon the quality of the work of the trades that precede it. If the foundation is not level, the walls won't be plumb. And if the walls aren't plumb, the doors and windows won't operate properly, etc. We saw in the first several chapters of this book where a theology constructed on top of a skewed foundation of divine election and predestination ultimately leads to a deity who has little resemblance to the God of Scripture.

In the construction industry, there is a running joke among contractors that when the architects and engineers design something that doesn't quite work, where the parts don't join together properly, their solution is simply to write a note on the plans that says, "P.T.F."—"Pound to Fit." In other words, do whatever it takes to make it work. There is a sense in which the distorted understanding of the doctrine of election has caused theologians to have to "pound to fit" in order to make other important Christian doctrines harmonize with their misunderstanding of divine election. Then they try to convince us that we're just going to have to live with windows that stick, plumbing that clogs, and a roof that leaks. I propose that is not the nature of the house that God built.

In this chapter we're going to examine what happens when we construct our theological "house" to allow a true biblical understanding of the doctrine of election to shape and inform some other critical doctrines of our Christian faith. A theology constructed on a firm foundation should generate a structure that doesn't need us to toil and strain to fit the pieces together. A theology built on the strong and stable foundation of the truth should develop naturally, assembling itself organically, into a beautiful house—a sound, viable structure able to withstand intellectual scrutiny and any winds of false doctrine. The various parts should fit without having to bend and twist and contort and pound on them. That is to say, we need to let God build the house, lest we labor in vain (Ps. 127:1).

Truth-seeking

In Chapter Four, I expressed three important implications of the biblical understanding that the elect in the New Testament writings were from a single generation, contemporary with the apostles. First, there is the awareness that we have been asking the wrong question. Our propensity to inject ourselves into the first-century context has caused us to focus on the completely irrelevant question, "Who *are* the elect?" rather than the relevant and appropriate biblical question, "Who *were* the elect?" Second, I assured that we are in really good company because none of the Old Testament heroes were of the elect, and neither were many of the New Testament saints. But that did not imply their eternal destruction—nor does not being part of the elect imply eternal damnation for us. Finally, we came to realize that since the doctrine of New Testament election was a unique first-century program initiated by God to launch the church, it has nothing to do with us at all. We can stop fretting over whether we and our loved ones are chosen or not. We're not, but that's okay. We're free to choose God. We're free from the burden imposed by a man-made teaching that has caused great division in the Christian ranks and, I believe, great harm to the cause of the kingdom.

If we allow the concept that New Testament election was restricted to the first century, and that no one is (or ever was) chosen by God specifically to go to heaven—if we allow that truth to ripple through our Christian traditions—we begin to see that there are profound repercussions to some of our popular understandings and begin to realize that the depth of disruptive wrong-thinking has caused to some traditional Christian ideologies. But wrong is wrong. As Christians guided by the Spirit of truth, we should be willing to go wherever the truth leads.

I've chosen three popular traditional Christian doctrines which have been built on a faulty foundation of a distorted view of the doctrine of election and predestination, resulting in a corrupted understanding of the gospel. The three traditional doctrines we'll examine are: (1) futurism; (2) "once saved always saved"/eternal security; and (3) total depravity/total inability.

Past or Future?

> But when you see Jerusalem surrounded by armies, then know that its desolation has come near. Then let those who are in Judea flee to the mountains, and let those who are inside the city depart, and let not those who are out in the country enter it, for these are days of vengeance, to fulfill all that is written.
>
> (Luke 21:20–22)

As a young Christian, I read all sixteen of the *Left Behind* books. I was captivated by the idea of a church that is raptured prior to a period of great tribulation and the dispensational notion of a future seven-year period where new Christian converts—the newly revealed elect—would be persecuted in a world that is run by a cabal of Satanic minions. Then, of course, comes the wonderful scene where Jesus returns and sets everything right... at least, until it all goes bad again. The problem is, such a scenario is not supported by the Bible.

It is common for some evangelical churches today to view many scriptures as end-time prophesies. Much of Daniel 9, Matthew 24, Matthew 25, Mark 13, Luke 17, Luke 21, and the entire book of Revelation are often seen as eschatological—that is, part of the study of "last things." In other words, they take a *futurist* view of these scriptures. However, there are others who view many of the same scriptures as describing events that have already been fulfilled. Most commonly, these *preterists* see the events described in these passages as having been fulfilled by the destruction of the temple by the Roman army in AD 70.

The genesis of the dispute between these two views seems to hinge on the understanding of a period referenced in Scripture as a time of "great tribulation." In Matthew 24, in the Olivet Discourse, Jesus refers to such a time. "For then there will be great tribulation, such as has not been from the beginning of the world until now, no, and never will be" (Matt. 24:21). Most futurists see this verse as describing catastrophic events related to the judgments in the book of Revelation—events that will occur in the years immediately prior to the second coming of Christ. Most preterists believe that Jesus was describing the persecution and suffering that would occur during the Jewish-Roman War from AD 66 to AD 70. Many volumes have been written by both camps citing their reasons for their beliefs, yet both cannot be right.

Stating the Obvious

In the verses that immediately follow his mention of the time of great tribulation, Jesus refers to "the elect" twice.

> And if those days had not been cut short, no human being would be saved. But for the sake of the elect those days will be cut short. Then if anyone says to you, "Look, here is the Christ!" or "There he is!" do not believe it. For false christs and false prophets will arise and perform great signs and wonders, so as to lead astray, if possible, even the elect. (Matt. 24:22–24)

With the understanding that New Testament election was restricted to a unique group of people from the first century, the debate regarding whether the time of great tribulation referred to in the Olivet Discourse in Matthew 24 is a future or a past event dissolves into the obvious. Since there are no such "elect" people beyond the first century, Jesus must be telling his disciples about an event which will occur in their lifetime, during "this generation." There are several compelling reasons to believe that in Matthew 24:21, the time of "great tribulation" was indeed a reference to the Jewish-Roman War, which ended with the siege of Jerusalem and the destruction of the temple.

First, in verse 2 of Matthew 24, Jesus tells his disciples of the coming destruction of the temple. In the verses that follow, Jesus describes a series of harbingers that will precede this event. The culmination of these warning signs is the "abomination of desolation," described by Luke as a time when Jerusalem will be surrounded by armies (Luke 21:20). We know from various historical records that Roman armies invaded Judea and the neighboring regions in AD 66, finally surrounding Jerusalem and destroying the temple in

AD 70—which would serve to fulfill Jesus's prophesy regarding the abomination of desolation (Matt. 24:15).

Second, historical documentation of the Jewish War describes a holocaust of epic proportions. The Roman army slaughtered more than a million Jews and enslaved nearly 100,000 of the survivors.[13] At the same time there was strife and infighting among the Jewish people, with some twelve thousand of Jerusalem's leading citizens tortured and killed by Zealots. Josephus, the Jewish author and historian, writes this eyewitness account:

> The noise also of those that were fighting was incessant, both by day and by night; but the lamentation of those that mourned exceeded the other (i.e., the noise of the fighting).... They, moreover, were still inventing somewhat or other that was pernicious against themselves; and when that had resolved upon anything, they execute it without mercy, and omitted no method of torment or of barbarity.[14]

And if the slaughter by the Romans and the internal strife were not tribulation enough, the siege of the city of Jerusalem occurred during the Passover season, when the city had swelled to many times its normal Jewish population. This served to exacerbate an already severe and desperate time of famine. Again, Josephus writes:

> The madness of the seditious did also increase together with their famine, and both those miseries were everyday inflamed more and more.... It was now a miserable case, and a sight that would justly bring tears into our eyes... insomuch that children pulled the very morsels that their

fathers were eating out of their very mouths... so did the mothers do as their infants.

Then did the famine widen its progress, and devoured the people by whole houses and families; and the lanes of the city were full of the dead bodies of the aged; the children also and the young men wandered about the market places like shadows, all swelled with the famine, and fell down dead wheresoever their misery seized them.... Thus did the miseries of Jerusalem grow worse and worse every day... And indeed the multitude of carcasses that lay in heaps one upon another, was a horrible sight, and produced a pestilential stench, which was a hinderance to those that would make sallies out of the city and fight the enemy... and those that were slain more in number than those who slew them; for the ground did nowhere appear visible because of the dead bodies that lay on it.[15]

It's hard to image a greater time of tribulation for the Jewish people than the three-and-a-half year period of the Jewish-Roman War, which would fulfill Jesus's prediction of a time of great distress and of "wars and rumors of wars" (Matt. 24:6).

Third, history records that in late AD 66, the Roman commander Cestius, for reasons unknown, suddenly withdrew his troops and temporarily halted the invasion.[16] This surprising turn of events gave Jewish believers the opportunity to flee the region unimpeded, heeding the advice of Jesus thirty-three years earlier to "flee to the mountains" (Luke 21:21). There are several extrabiblical sources recounting a mass exodus of Jewish Christians fleeing Jerusalem to the village of Pella in Perea, east of the Jordan River.[17] Then, as prophesied by Jesus several decades earlier, "for the sake of the elect," those days of great tribulation were cut short. In AD 70, the city was torched, the temple completely destroyed, and the siege ended. There are reports that, unexplainably, no Christians died in the genocidal holocaust of the Jewish-Roman War.

Final Thoughts on Futurism

When we construct our understanding of the Olivet Discourse (and other passages traditionally considered to be eschatological) on the firm foundation of the true-to-the-Bible concept that New Testament election was a first-century doctrine with no direct application for future generations, the pieces begin to fit together seamlessly. There is no need to manipulate the text, as some do, to justify an interpretation that "soon" didn't really mean soon, that "near" didn't really mean imminent, or that "this generation" was really a reference to some group of people thousands of years in the future. Our true-to-Scripture understanding of the doctrine of election affirms a preterist (past) view of the Olivet Discourse, and resolves the long-standing argument between futurists and preterists caused, in part, by a misinterpretation of the doctrine of election.

Once Saved, Always Saved?

> *For false christs and false prophets will arise and perform great signs and wonders, so as to lead astray, if possible, even the elect.*
>
> (*Matthew 24:24*)

A local pastor used to tell of a guy on his college campus that always wore a t-shirt with the word "GOD" imprinted in large, bold letters on it. While it is not likely that he convinced anyone that he was

really God, in the first century, history records instances of oppor-
tunists and false prophets claiming to be Jesus, or claiming to know
of the Messiah's whereabouts, taking advantage of the chaos and
grief surrounding the Jewish community in Judea immediately after
the catastrophic events of the Jewish-Roman War.[18] Jesus warned his
disciples that such would be the case, "so as to lead astray, if possible,
even the elect" (Matt. 24:24).

Matthew 24:24 has been used to defend a doctrine commonly
known as eternal security, or "once saved, always saved" (OSAS).
Simply put, OSAS is the belief that God will not let a true Christian
fall away from the faith. Not surprisingly, the same verse has been
used to *deny* this doctrine as well. Both camps cite the phrase "if
possible" as evidence for their understanding of the doctrine.

Is it possible for a true Christian to fall away (or be led away)
from the faith? At the root of this centuries-old controversy regarding eternal security is the lack of a clear understanding of the doctrine of election. When we recognize that God's plan for the early
church was not "one size fits all," and that the Bible makes a distinction between the way God worked in the apostles, the way God
worked in the elect, and the way God works in today's Christian, the
same question could yield different answers. Therefore, three questions are necessary: 1) Was it possible for the elect to fall away from
the faith? 2) Is it possible for true Christians in today's church to fall
away from the faith? and 3) Could an apostle have fallen away from
the faith?

In my biblical model of the gospel in Chapter Five, I defined the
apostles and the elect as unique subsets of Christian disciples, yet
distinct from each other. The melding together of all believers into
a single classification in much of today's thinking confuses the issue
of election, blurs the understanding of eternal security, and obscures
the beautiful clarity and masterful unfolding of God's plan to save

the world through his Son, Jesus Christ. The apostles were divinely enabled to replace Jesus as God's messengers and to gather the elect. The elect were uniquely chosen to receive the gospel message from the apostles and divinely gifted for the specific task of initiating the church. The church is to carry on God's soul-saving business, growing in faith and persuading the unbelieving world of the truth of the gospel. Three different entities—three different purposes in God's plan—three potentially different answers to this question about eternal security.

1. Was it possible for the elect to fall away from the faith?

The New Testament presents salvation as conditional for all believers. The required condition is a persevering faith in Jesus Christ. This truth is supported by the many exhortations throughout the New Testament which encourage the believer to "strive to enter that rest" (Heb. 4:11), to endure to the end (Rev. 3:10), to "continue in the faith" (Col. 1:23), and "hold fast our confession" (Heb. 4:14). The implication is that the gift of faith is precious, but fragile, and the believer must work to nurture, strengthen, and preserve his faith. Additionally, there are a number of unsettling verses which seem to predict the apostasy (falling away) of believers, clearly warning that "some will depart from the faith" (1 Tim. 4:1), and that those who have "fallen away" cannot be brought back to repentance (Heb. 6:6).

With the understanding that everything presented in the epistles of the New Testament was written "for the sake of the elect" (2 Tim. 2:10; Titus 1:1), we can know that all of the exhortations to persevere in the faith and all biblical counsel against falling away were sincere and dire warnings against apostasy directed at God's chosen people. Furthermore, because the elect had received the unmistakable imprimatur of God, were given the honor of representing him, and were critical to the success of God's salvific plan, we read of the potential for severe judgment for those who fall away after receiving the knowledge of the truth. The writer of Hebrews, after encouraging the elect Jews to "hold fast the confession of our hope" (Heb. 10:23), issues a warning to those who were tempted to leave the faith and return to the ways of the old covenant.

> How much worse punishment, do you think, will be deserved by the one who has trampled underfoot the Son of God, and has profaned the blood of the covenant by which he was sanctified, and has outraged the Spirit of grace? (Heb. 10:29)

I previously cited the passage in Hebrews 6 which, I believe, addresses the apostasy of the elect, indicating that their falling away would be "crucifying once again the Son of God to their own harm and holding him up to contempt" (Heb. 6:6). The writer decries the act of apostasy of these blessed servants as a betrayal—an act which would not only subject Christ to public shame but would be comparable to a recrucifying of the Son of God.

In sum, despite their advantage of being chosen and divinely gifted, apostasy is viewed by the writers of the New Testament as a very real concern, even for the elect.

2. Is it possible for true Christians in today's church to fall away from the faith?

When we consider that even God's elect were warned with great passion and sincere concern about the reality of apostasy, how then can we, the nonelect Christians, justify a doctrine which denies the possibility of apostasy for us? In his classic treatise on the doctrine of perseverance, *Life in the Son*, Robert Shank states, "Completely absurd is the assumption that men are to be sincerely persuaded that apostasy is impossible, and at the same time, sincerely alarmed at the warnings."[19] Indeed, the warnings are many, and a search of the Scriptures does not yield a single verse that guarantees salvation, neither for the elect nor for non-elect Christian.

This is not to say that God hasn't "stacked the deck" to help his children succeed in persevering in the faith. The somewhat enigmatic, co-laboring aspect of salvation is presented by Paul in his letter to the elect in the church at Philippi.

> Therefore, my beloved, as you have always obeyed, so now, not only as in my presence but much more in my absence, work out your own salvation with fear and trembling, for it is God who works in you, both to will and to work for his good pleasure. (Phil. 2:12—13)

It is clear that only those who strive, endure, continue, persevere, and overcome will be saved. There's no doubt that we can count on the help of a God who loves us and who is "for us," but we must heed the same warnings issued by the apostles to God's elect.

3. Could an apostle have fallen away from the faith?

As we page through the New Testament, we see passages which clearly state that there were people who seemed to be guaranteed salvation. Jesus speaks of those whom he will "never cast out" (John 6:37) but will "raise him up on the last day" (John 6:40), and of those whom "no one can snatch out of [his] hand" (John 10:28). How do we reconcile those promises with the understanding that apostasy was a viable concern for the elect and is still possible for

Christians today? Let's look at a passage often used to defend the doctrine of OSAS.

> My sheep hear my voice, and I know them, and they follow me. I give them eternal life, and they will never perish, and no one will snatch them out of my hand. My Father, who has given them to me, is greater than all, and no one is able to snatch them out of the Father's hand. (John 10:27—29)

These "red-letter" verses in the Gospel of John clearly state a guarantee that for Jesus' sheep, salvation is secure. So how do we harmonize the truth of this promise of eternal life with the clear teaching that apostasy for God's chosen people is real? The key is in the understanding of who Jesus considered to be "his sheep."

Sheep

In Chapter 10 of the Gospel of John, Jesus describes three groups of sheep: "the sheep," "my sheep," and "other sheep." Each group is defined by its role in the metaphor offered by Jesus in the Good Shepherd Discourse. Each group has distinct characteristics. I propose that these designations roughly correspond to the apostles, the elect, and the church. Jesus lays down his life for "the sheep"—the church. The "my sheep" group knows him, hears his voice, and follows him. Additionally, Jesus defines this group as those who were "given to him by the Father." These, I propose, were the twelve Jewish men given to Jesus to disciple—the apostles. Still, Jesus has "other sheep"—the elect—comprised of Jews and Gentiles, who were not originally part of his flock but will also hear his voice and join in, so that there will be "one flock, one shepherd" (John 10:16).

Note that the only group with the assurance of salvation, those who cannot be snatched out of Jesus's hand (or the Father's hand) is the "my sheep" group, those "given to him by the Father." Contrary to popular teaching, there is only one group of people Jesus ever refers to as "his sheep." In fulfillment of the prophesy in Ezekiel 34, the apostles had been chosen to become God's representatives of the nation of Israel, a faithful remnant, the sheep of God. The shepherd sought them out (Ezek. 34:11) and chose them (John 15:16). Again, it is only when we blur the distinction between the church, the elect, and the apostles—lumping them together into a single, one-size-fits-all singularity—that we mistakenly attribute the unique graces given to the apostles to all Christians, causing confusion and contradictions.

Given by the Father

On the night of his arrest, Jesus informed his Father that he had completed the work he was given to do (John 17:3), which he defined as manifesting the Father's name to those given to him: "I have manifested your name to the people whom you gave me out of the world. Yours they were, and you gave them to me, and they have kept your word" (John 17:6).

In the passage above, Jesus twice refers to those with him in the upper room, the eleven remaining apostles, as those given to him by the Father. I propose that the phrase, "those given to him by the Father" (or similar wording) is an expositional constant—that is, always an allusion to the apostles. This distinctive phrase is only uttered nine times in Scripture, all in the gospel of John. Its conspicuous absence throughout the New Testament letters reveals that this manner of coming to Jesus—being given by the Father—was a unique, pre-cross process which is never employed by God subsequent to Jesus's earthly ministry. If being given to Jesus by the Father were a normative process for believers to become Christians, it seems odd that such an important theological concept is not found anywhere in the epistles from Paul, Peter, or John, nor is it found in the books of Acts or Hebrews.

It seems logical to conclude that those who were given to Jesus by the Father were those who were appointed to join Jesus in his earthly ministry. Note that when Jesus says, "All that the Father gives me will come to me" (John 6:37), he does not necessarily imply that those given to him will come *to believe* in him, but rather that they will come to be *with* him. So, while it is clear from Scripture that no one comes to the Father except through Jesus (John 14:6), what is not supported is a universal soteriological concept where no one comes to Jesus except through the Father. The biblical process of coming to faith in Jesus as presented consistently in the New Testament writings—the way you and I came to believe—is always via the power of the gospel and the working of the Holy Spirit. From this we can conclude that being given to Jesus by the Father was a unique, divine appointment for a special uniting of the apostles with Jesus—not a normative soteriological process.

I'm aware that the above argumentation regarding those given to Jesus by the Father is not definitive or conclusive, but when taken along with grammatical and contextual clues found in the nine passages that reference the giving of people to Jesus by the Father, the most logical explanation is that only the apostles were in view. So, although it is God's will that "everyone who looks on the Son and believes in him should have eternal life, and [be raised] up on the last day" (John 6:40), the condition for salvation has always been perseverance of faith in Jesus, without exception. The apostles, however, were uniquely blessed, distinct from all other disciples, in that they seemed to have a divine and prophetic guarantee of being held in faith to the end. In a promise made only to the apostles, Jesus prophesied that they would one day be in heaven sitting on twelve thrones judging the twelve tribes of Israel (Matt. 19:28; Luke 22:30). The faithful fulfillment of this prophesy is the only guaranteed promise of salvation offered to any specific individuals in the pages of Scripture.

Final Thoughts on the Doctrine of Once Saved, Always Saved

Could the apostles have fallen away from the faith? The question of eternal security regarding the apostles is unanswerable because it dwells in the true mystery between predictive prophesy and libertarian free will. In the end, an accurate understanding of the doctrine of election reveals that, even though both the apostles and the elect were chosen by God and graced with special gifts to help them launch the church, neither their election nor their gifting was a guarantee of their ultimate destiny. Eternal life has always been conditioned on abiding faithfulness, and even though the apostle Paul tells us that the elect were chosen as "firstfruits to be saved" (2 Tim. 2:23), it was not a guarantee of eternal life, only a confirmation that they were the first generation with the opportunity for salvation through the "sanctifying work of the Spirit" and "belief in the truth" (2 Thess. 2:13). There were no exceptions to the obligation to abide in Christ for eternal life—not for the apostles, not for the elect, and not for us. Our security as Christians rests in the faithfulness of God.

Total Inability?

> *Choose life.*
>
> *(Deuteronomy 30:19)*

One day in my high school English class, we were asked to write a two-page essay. The following day we were required to condense our two-page essay into a single paragraph, then into a single sentence, and finally into a single word. The purpose of the assignment was to illustrate the power of "essential brevity." Jesus illustrated the concept brilliantly when he condensed the entire Old Testament—the Law and the Prophets, all 23,135 verses—into two simple verses:

> "Teacher, which is the great commandment in the Law?" And he said to him, "You shall love the Lord your God with all your heart and with all your soul and with all your mind. This is the great and first commandment. And a second is like it: You shall love your neighbor as yourself." (Matt. 22:36—39)

Then, Jesus makes the astounding statement that all of the Law and the Prophets *depend* on these two commandments (v. 40). At the heart of the Hebrew scriptures—the Law and the Prophets—is the revealing of God's plan to save the world through his Son, Jesus Christ. What Jesus is clearly saying is that the entire plan of salvation depends on love: our love for God, and our love for others. In other words God's eternal plan of salvation depends, in no small part, on us! Yet, the Reformed doctrine of total depravity proposes the biblically unsupportable notion that, by divine fiat, man is unable to love God—the very thing that Jesus says makes the gospel work!

I believe that the doctrine of total depravity/total inability is the foundational error upon which the faulty framing of Reformed theology is constructed. It is the flawed doctrine of total depravity that makes necessary the equally unbiblical Reformed doctrines of unconditional election and irresistible grace. Let's take a moment to define the doctrine of total depravity.

In his book *The Potter's Freedom*, James White defines total depravity like this:

> Man is dead in sin, completely and radically impacted by the Fall, the enemy of God, incapable of saving himself. This does not mean that man is as evil as he could be. Nor does it mean that the image of God is destroyed, or that the will is done away with. Instead, it refers to the all pervasiveness of the effects of sin, and the fact that man is, outside of Christ, the enemy of God.[20]

According to Reformed theology, since man is "dead" and an "enemy" of God, only an act of divine mercy (irresistible grace) on God's part can quicken him and give him the ability to respond positively to the gospel. And since we know that not everyone becomes a Christian, the Calvinists reason that God must have chosen only certain people (unconditional election) upon whom to bestow this saving grace. But if, as I propose, no individual was chosen specifically for salvation by God and no one is irresistibly imbued with a saving faith, yet many come to believe in the gospel message, there must be another mechanism by which a saving faith is acquired—something other than divine election and irresistible grace. That mechanism is love.

In the first chapter of this book, we saw where the Reformed view of election rendered God's love completely unrecognizable. Some Calvinist scholars were forthright and admitted that God really doesn't love everyone. Others maintain that God does indeed love everyone, even the reprobate, but does not offer them the salvific love necessary to obtain eternal life. As evidence of God's "love" for all, they often refer to a "general call" of the gospel, an insincere offer to all to come to Jesus and, as further evidence of God's love for the nonelect, they often cite Matthew 5:45: "he makes his sun rise on the evil and on the good, and sends rain on the just and on the unjust." Roger Olson, in his book *Against Calvinism*, reflected on such a "love" and opined that in Calvinism, "God provides the nonelect with a little bit of heaven to go to hell in."[21]

In the debate regarding divine election, it is unfortunate that God's beautiful, steadfast love for his creation often gets obscured beneath layers of overanalysis and confusing intellectual rhetoric. The Bible tells us simply, "We love because he first loved us" (1 John 4:19). So the grace that allows us to love God and love others (we can call it prevenient grace, if you like) is really God's relationship-initiating love and the divine enablement of a critical, image-bearing attribute in his creatures—the ability to love. Let's define love for God, and love for others.

Love for God

I confess that I spent much of my early Christian years worried that I didn't love God. I saw others in church with arms raised, eyes closed, enrapt in song or prayer. They seemed to love God way beyond what I felt for God. In my mind was the thought, "How can anyone—even God—*command* love from another?" And if it's commanded, is it really love that's given in return? Or is it something else?

Somewhere along my Christian walk, I came across the following verse and, as God would have it, the truth set me free; "For this is the love of God, that we keep his commandments. And his commandments are not burdensome" (1 John 5:3). Love for God is defined simply as obedience to God—obedience with a good attitude. Suddenly I realized that I had the ability to love God, and so does everyone else, not perfectly, of course, but we can certainly strive for perfect obedience. So when Jesus says that the great and first commandment is to love God, it is simply a command for intentional obedience.

Love for Others

In the quest for "essential brevity," Paul takes it a step further than Jesus did and condenses the Law down to one word/verse: "For the whole law is fulfilled in one word: 'You shall love your neighbor as yourself'" (Gal. 5:14). How can Paul reduce the whole law into just the single command to "love your neighbor as yourself'? He knows that by loving others (Jesus's second greatest commandment), we are also obeying the "great and first commandment": loving/obeying God. By God's own decree, our love for God is embedded in our love for others! With his teaching to the Galatians, Paul is actually restating Jesus's words in Matthew 7:12, "So whatever you wish that others would do to you, do also to them, for this is the Law and the Prophets."

In his final statement about the Law, I believe that Jesus crystallizes what it means to love others when he rebukes the Pharisees for neglecting "the weightier matters of the Law: justice, mercy, and faithfulness" (Matt. 23:23). So loving others—the fulfillment of the Law—can be understood as being dependable (faithfulness), and being fair (justice), and showing compassion (mercy). With this biblical definition of love, I believe that no rational-thinking person would deny that everyone has the ability to love others—that is, to be just, merciful, and faithful.

The Myth of Godlessness

The foundational flaw in the Reformed doctrine of total depravity becomes evident when we connect the dots and realize that by loving others, we are actually loving God—the very thing the Reformed doctrine proposes we cannot do. The recognition that everyone, without exception, has the ability to love is all the evidence we need to know that the godless man proposed by the doctrine of total depravity is a myth with no biblical basis. Even John Calvin maintained that actual godlessness is an impossibility when he declares,

> Men of sound judgment will always be sure that a sense of divinity which can never be effaced, is engraved upon men's minds... there is some God... naturally inborn in all, and is fixed deep within, as if it were the very marrow.[22]

One final point of clarification regarding the belief that God has given everyone, without exception, the ability to love. A Calvinist might argue with regard to motive: unless the love comes from a place of worship/devotion to God, they would aver, it has no kingdom value. To this argument I would say that there is only One who loved perfectly. No one ascribes every good deed to God. No one loves perfectly. Yet, all do good deeds. All display love. So with regard to the unbeliever, motive is largely irrelevant. God has simply enabled every person to love by first loving them.

What about Unconditional Election and Irresistible Grace?

Individuals are unconditionally chosen in the Bible. Individuals are irresistibly enabled in the Bible. But while it's true that we see both of these doctrines in Scripture, contrary to the Reformed understanding, neither the election nor the grace were manifestations of a secure eternal destiny—neither in the Old Testament nor in the New. That is not to say that being chosen and enabled by God would not have provided a salvific advantage. For example, Paul describes the great advantages given to the nation of Israel as God's chosen people in Romans 9:4–5, yet only by the faithfulness of the individual could salvation be achieved (Matt. 24:13; Col. 1:22–23).

Below is a chart illustrating the *biblical* (not Reformed) concepts of unconditional election, irresistible grace and total depravity in the New Testament.

	Apostles	Elect	Nonelect Christians
Total Depravity/Total Inability	No	No	No
Unconditional Election	Yes	Yes	No
Irresistible Grace	Yes	Yes	No

With regard to unconditional election:

- The apostles were chosen unconditionally (with no reason given for the particular election of any individual) to be trained to replace Jesus as God's new ambassadors.

- The elect were chosen unconditionally (with no reason given for the particular election of any individual) to carry on the work of the apostles.

- The nonelect Christians were/are not chosen.

With regard to irresistible grace:

- The apostles received (irresistibly) the grace that revealed Jesus as the Messiah and the gifting to be effective ministers to the elect.

- The elect received (irresistibly) the grace to believe the message of the apostles and the gifting required to be effective in launching the church.

- The nonelect were/are not graced with kingdom service gifts in a like manner as the apostles and the elect.

With regard to total depravity/total inability:

- No one has ever been unable to love/obey/know God, with a few notable and rare exceptions:

  - where God has *temporarily* blinded them for his divine purposes (Mark 4:11–12);

  - where God has judicially hardened them in judgment for "refusing to love the truth" (2 Thess. 2:10); or

  - for their persistent and inexcusable unbelief (Rom. 1:20; 11:20).

Final Thoughts on the Doctrine of Total Depravity

When God explained the punishment to Adam and Eve for their disobedience in Genesis 3, there was no mention of spiritual separation from God, no mention of man's inability to love/obey/know God, no mention of spiritual deadness nor any other significant change in the relationship between man and God. In regard to the Reformed doctrine of total depravity, George W. Burnap observes, "If this doctrine is true, God did not tell man the true penalty, neither the truth, nor the whole truth, nor a hundredth part of the truth."[23]

The Reformed concept of total depravity is unsupportable in Scripture. The doctrine of election, as proposed in this book, recognizes the absence of scriptural support for the Reformed proposal that God has rendered man unable to love him—the very attribute necessary for the success of the gospel. The true, biblical doctrine of election, as illustrated in this book, proposes that everyone, without exception, has always been given the capacity to overcome their sinful nature, the grace to love God, and the ability to call on his name and be saved.

8

FINALLY, GOD

What comes into our minds when we think about God is the most important thing about us.

—A. W. Tozer[24]

God. Who he is; *that* he is; what he is like; and what we mere mortals must do about him—this is what A. W. Tozer refers to as "the overwhelming problem of God."[25] He goes on to say that every error in doctrine and every failure in Christian ethics can be attributed to "imperfect and ignoble" thoughts of God. They not only lead to idolatry—they are idolatry itself. Unfortunately, such idolatry can be found in many churches today. For example, some churches teach us to think about God as "the One who chooses," when the cross teaches us that God is "the One who loves." And some churches have led us to believe that God's glory means everything to him, when the cross teaches that he sacrificed his glory to save us.

It is somewhat confounding to think that scholars have spent centuries going to battle over a completely inconsequential, and largely irrelevant doctrine in today's Christianity. It's painful to realize that many, many truth-seeking people have been ostracized (and worse) for questioning a man-corrupted doctrine, yet one taught as though of God. And it's painful to acknowledge that I had spent more than a decade fretting about the doctrine of election and predestination—in part because I, like every other serious Christian, wanted whatever God wants. Yet, the simple biblical truth about election achieves two of God's primary goals: it is both glorifying to God and personally liberating for those who believe in the truth of God's word. And the truth is, when the writers of the New Testament speak of the elect, they are referring to a group of first-century individuals, chosen by God, divinely enabled to receive the gospel as presented by the apostles, and uniquely gifted to effectively launch the church. I am not one of the elect. I am a post-election Christian, and that will suffice.

Don't Look Back

I have heard that a horse, after being led out of a burning barn, will sometimes, for reasons not clear, break loose and head back into the burning structure. For similar reasons not clear, I fear there will be a desire by many to break loose from the liberating understanding that there is no relevant doctrine of election for today's Christian and head back into the bondage of Calvinism or Arminianism or some other doctrinal -ism. With the abandonment of a centuries-old error in the application of election comes the uneasy feeling that there is now a huge hole in traditional Christianity—and perhaps there is. The truth that New Testament election was a first-century strategy with no direct application for today's Christian allowed us to unravel the Calvinistic doctrines of total depravity, irresistible grace, and unconditional election. We also resolve the debate between futurists and preterists because we eliminate the error of believing that divine election is a normative process of salvation. And we lose the false idea that simply walking the aisle, praying a prayer, or throwing a pine cone into the fire at junior high school church camp while professing belief that Jesus is the Savior is a guarantee of salvation—the once-saved-always-saved fallacy.

It is unfortunate that so much of our religion has been tied to, and filled with, man-created doctrines which blur the beauty and clarity of biblical truths. Jesus once rebuked Peter for "not setting [his] mind on things of God, but on things of man" (Matt. 16:23), and warned his disciples against those who pass off man-made doctrines as divine.

> This people honors me with their lips, but their heart is far from me; in vain do they worship me, teaching as doctrines the commandments of men. (Matt. 15:8–9)

It may be somewhat unfair to harshly judge centuries of scholars who were futilely contemplating divine doctrines with human sensibilities, yet I can't help but feel that, out of desperation to find answers, many theologians were willing to accept implausible explanations for perceived biblical mysteries and failed to notice that they had veered far from the image of the true God of the Bible and his gracious plan of salvation. They preoccupied themselves with intellectual contemplation when God was desiring simple adoration. Or, as A. W. Tozer explained, they were busy being theologians when God was simply seeking saints.[26]

The absence of a contemporary application for the doctrine of election may have left a hole in our traditional religion, but rushing in to fill the void is the comfort and power of God's grace. My conclusion that no one today is chosen by God specifically for salvation has a necessary corollary: no one today is *excluded* by God specifically *from* salvation. So I guess it would be accurate to state that, in a way, God has chosen *everyone* specifically for salvation. While the Bible is filled with people in the past who were chosen to fulfill various purposes in God's plan, the offer to receive the grace that leads to eternal life has always been available to all, with rare and warranted exceptions. With this confidence, we can approach anyone with the assurance of God's love and a sincere offer of hope that the saving atonement accomplished on the cross can be personally applied by whosoever places their faith in Jesus.

Closing

> *And he took [the little children] in his arms and blessed them, laying his hands on them. (Mark 10:16)*

In the tenth chapter of the gospel of Mark, we get the beautiful and touching scene when Jesus draws a group of little children close to him and blesses them. He doesn't express any worries about which ones are able to come to him and which ones are not, which ones were chosen from before the foundation of the world for salvation and which of these little children were predestined to perish. There's no indication that he looked down the corridors of time to determine which of these beautiful children would become Christians and which would resist the Spirit of truth. He gathers all of them to himself and blesses them all. He knows that, because of the cross, eternal life will be available to every child, and that after the cross, every one of them—and all future generations of children—will be drawn to Him with the God-given ability to seek him, reach out for him, and find him, because he will never be far from each and every one of them. That's the true, biblical gospel!

In the same way, we don't have to carry the burden of worrying that maybe our loved ones might have been predestined for destruction, without hope, unable to come to Jesus by the decree of God. We can confidently tell our family members, friends, and children that God loves them and died for them, knowing that God doesn't want any of them to perish, and that he's working on their behalf to help them succeed. And to our believing friends and family members we can say with confidence that they are right where they're supposed to be—abiding in Jesus, as members of his church. They are the bride of Christ, loved by God, desired by God, heirs to the kingdom, free, forgiven, and blessed.

Finally, with the words of A. W. Tozer haunting me (actually, more taunting me) to be sure that God is getting a saint and not just a theologian, I offer this exhortation: do not "ignore so great a salvation" (Heb. 2:3), and "Do not neglect to do good and to share what you have, for such sacrifices are pleasing to God" (Heb. 13:16). It is my hope that by coming to a true-to-the-Bible understanding of the doctrine of election, we can all stop with the "foolish quarrels" (2 Tim. 2:23) that so destructively divide the body of Christ. It is my hope that we can all get back to simply loving and worshipping God, and loving and serving others—which is the real business of life.

AFTERWORD

[D]o not be anxious about anything, but in everything by prayer and supplication with thanksgiving let your requests be made known to God.

(Philippians 4:6)

One day, while driving north on the busy 405 freeway in Southern California, my wife turned to me with a pensive look on her face and asked, "How much does a billboard cost?" The minute she posed the question that day, I knew what she had in mind: How much would it cost to rent billboard space on a busy interstate and write a simple message in large letters, "PRAY FOR OUR SON"?

I began this book with a short accounting of how I believe that God arranged events in my life to lead me on a journey to find a noncontradictory, biblically supportable understanding of the doctrine of election. One of the primary motives for embarking on such a journey was the difficulties with my own son's drug addiction and rebellion. Does God love him? Did Jesus die for him? He was nineteen years old and facing years in prison. My wife and I had exhausted our own resources and abandoned any thought that we, in our own strength, had any real power to make a difference

121

in his future. Despite all of our efforts—which included various rehab programs, clinical evaluations, counseling sessions, behavior contracts, and interventions—nothing seemed to have an impact on the downward spiral of his life.

After years of struggle, in desperation and with nowhere else to turn, we turned to God, with the intention to give our son over to Him. I prayed, "warning" God of our plan to hand our son over. Immediately after that decision it was as if I could hear God's still, small voice saying to us, "It's about time. I'll take it from here." One of the side effects of trusting God with our precious son was the complete loss of parental pride. Even though we had long ago abandoned any notion that we had any chance of being nominated for "parents of the year," letting go of control and admitting powerlessness was still quite humbling.

Driven by love, my wife set out on a crusade to get as many people as possible to pray for him. She was bold and assertive, approaching anyone she thought might believe in the true God, and asking for prayer for our son and for us. Any pride and any shame she might have felt was completely swallowed up in her boundless love for him.

Even though we did not follow through with the billboard idea, the army of faithful prayer warriors that she enlisted was busy at work, interceding for us and appealing to God on our son's behalf. Again, I almost felt that I needed to warn God of the deluge of prayers he would be receiving to heal our son.

To make a long story short: although things got really tough at first, both for him and for us, we knew in our hearts that God was at work. By God's grace, Johnny avoided the twenty-five-to-life sentence and was released after serving five years. God continued to bless him. He found a career for which he has a passion and aptitude; he found a girl he loves; and, through all the hardships, he found a God who loves him and a Savior who died for him.

As I write this epilogue, Johnny has been out of prison, clean and sober, for about seven years. He's happily married and excelling in his trade. We praise God every day for the grace he has shown. There is no way we can properly express the gratitude we feel to all of those people who prayed for him (and for us) during those difficult years, except to let them know that we truly believe that their prayers saved the life and soul of a truly remarkable young man and strengthened the faith of a grateful mother and father. Their faithfulness restored our sincere belief that God is the One who loves, not the One who chooses.

ENDNOTES

[1] Warren Wiersbe, *The Bible Exposition Commentary, New Testament, Volume 2* (Colorado Springs: Victor Books, 2001), 11.

[2] C. S. Lewis, *The Case for Christianity* (New York: Simon & Schuster, 1996), 42.

[3] John Wesley, *John Wesley*, edited by Albert C. Outler (New York: Oxford University Press, 1964), 447.

[4] John Piper, "What Is Your Capacity for Mystery? Exploring the Tension between Calvinists and Arminians," Desiring God, May 13, 2015, https://www.desiringgod.org/articles/what-is-your-capacity-for-mystery.

[5] John MacArthur, "John MacArthur: Calvinism vs. Arminianism," YouTube video, 6:00, April 11, 2018, https://www.youtube.com/watch?v=VEH-X2rP0WM.

[6] C. S. Lewis, *The Problem of Pain* (New York: The Century Press, 1940), 18.

[7] R. C. Sproul, "What Is Free Will? Chosen by God with R. C. Sproul," YouTube video, 30:14, Ligonier Ministries, April 23, 2015, https://www.youtube.com/watch?v=bcyttnC6cjg.

[8] "The (unbreakable) golden chain of redemption/salvation" is a common term for the sequence described by the apostle Paul in Romans 8:29–30.

[9] John Calvin, *Institutes of the Christian Religion*, Book III, paragraph 5.

[10] C. S. Lewis, *Christian Reflections* (New York: Harper One, 1967), 12, 16.

[11] John Piper, "How Does a Sovereign God Love?" Desiring God, February 1, 1983, https://www.desiringgod.org/articles/how-does-a-sovereign-god-love.

[12] C. S. Lewis, *Mere Christianity* (Samizdat, 2014; orig. 1952), 67; http://www.samizdat.qc.ca/vc/pdfs/MereChristianity_CSL.pdf.

[13] Josephus, *The Wars of the Jews*, Book 6, Chapter 9.3.

[14] Josephus, *The Wars of the Jews*, Book 6, Chapter 1.5.

[15] Josephus, *The Wars of the Jews*, Book 6, Chapter 5.1.

[16] Josephus, *The Wars of the Jews*, Book 6, Chapter 2.

[17] Josephus, *The Wars of the Jews*, Book 6, Chapter 18.

[18] Josephus, *The Wars of the Jews*, Book 7, Chapter 11.1.

[19] Robert Shank, *Life in the Son: A Study in the Doctrine of Perseverance* (Minneapolis: Bethany House Publishers, 1970), 172.

[20] James R. White, *The Potter's Freedom, A Defense of the Reformation and a Rebuttal of Norman Geisler's Chosen But Free* (Calvary Press, 2000), 39.

[21] Roger E. Olson, *Against Calvinism* (Grand Rapids, MI: Zondervan 2011), 139.

[22] Calvin, *Institutes of the Christian Religion*, 1559, i.33.

[23] George W. Burnap, "Lectures on the Doctrines of Christianity: in Controversy Between Unitarians and Other Denominations of Christians," 1835

[24] A. W. Tozer, *The Knowledge of the Holy* (New York: Harper Collins, 1961), 1.

[25] Tozer, 1.

[26] Tozer, 1.

ABOUT THE AUTHOR

John E. Chipman has earned and utilized a Master of Architecture degree, taught high school Spanish, played in a jazz/rock band, and currently teaches at The Spoken Word Christian Church in Southern California. John and his wife, Nancy, a beautiful and talented artist, have one adopted child who, coincidentally, is also married to a beautiful and talented artist.

Having studied architecture, music, art, math, and foreign languages at nine different colleges and universities, John Chipman's bio sounds like it describes someone who either could not decide what he wanted to be when he grew up or is intrigued and inspired by a variety of academic and intellectual challenges. He confesses to being guilty on both counts.

Through all his academic and business pursuits, John has come to realize that glorifying God by reflecting God's grace to others is the real business of life.